A LEVEL
Questions and Answers

D0493969

Q&A

PSYCHOLOGY

Cara Flanagan

Examiner

Letts

EDUCATIONAL

SERIES EDITOR: BOB McDUELL

Contents

Introduction

HOW TO USE THIS BOOK

The aim of the Questions and Answers series is to provide the student with the help required to attain the highest level in A- and AS-level Psychology.

It is designed to help all students up to grade A. The series relies on the idea that an experienced Examiner can provide (through examination questions, sample answers and advice) the help a student needs to secure success. It concentrates more on the examination skills necessary for a good grade rather than on factual information. The essays cover the most obvious and well-known material which would constitute an example grade A–A★ answer.

The **Questions and Answers** series is designed to provide:

- Easy-to-use **revision summaries** to remind you, in summary form, of the factual information you will need to have revised in order to answer the examination questions. The revision summaries in this book conform to the AEB syllabus exactly, and are followed by additional details for NEAB and OCSEB candidates. The last unit in the book (Applied and Contemporary Psychology) is for NEAB and OCSEB candidates, and contains those parts of their syllabuses not already covered.

- Many examples of **examination questions**. The AEB states that 'for each section of the syllabus there will be four questions in the examination, one from each sub-section of the subject content'. The same plan has been followed in this book so that there are four questions in each unit, one from each sub-section. Units 7 and 8 are slightly different. In the Perspectives unit there are only three sub-sections and three questions. In the Research Methods unit, there are several short structured questions.

- **Sample answers** to all questions. Most questions have been answered with a full essay. Some have been answered by an **outline answer**, which provides in outline form all the key information for a good answer. Answer each question yourself first and then compare your answer with the one provided here. Each sample answer is intended to be *typical* of grade A–A★ and to illustrate the necessary skills rather than being the 'right' answer.

- **Advice from the examiner**. Each answer starts with some **tips** about how to read and answer the question. At the end of the answer, and elsewhere when appropriate, there are further tips about how the answer would be marked. These should help you identify where marks are gained and where they can be lost.

THE IMPORTANCE OF USING QUESTIONS FOR REVISION

It is unlikely that any question you try will appear in exactly the same form on the papers you are going to take. However, the examiner is restricted on what can be set since questions must cover the whole syllabus and test certain Assessment Objectives. The number of totally original questions that can be set on any part of the syllabus is very limited and so similar ideas occur over and over again. It certainly will help you if the questions you are trying to answer in an examination are familiar and you know you have answered similar questions before. This is a great boost for your confidence and this is a key feature of exam success.

Practising examination questions will also highlight gaps in your knowledge which you can go back and revise more thoroughly. It will indicate the sort of questions you can do well and which, if there is a choice of questions, you should avoid. It will also help you with timing your answers, so you can work out how to pace yourself in the examination.

Attempting past questions will accustom you to the type of language which is used and help you learn to interpret it correctly.

Finally, having access to annotated answers, as you do in this book, will enable you to see clearly what is required by the examiner, how best to answer each question, and the amount of specific detail required.

MAXIMIZING YOUR MARKS

One of the keys to examination success is to know how marks are gained and lost by candidates. There are several important aspects to this.

Overall strategy

Where you have to answer four questions in three hours, this leaves you an average of 45 minutes on each essay question, including thinking/planning time. You might distribute your time differently, for example, spend 20 minutes deciding which questions to do and writing plans for each of them, and 10 minutes at the end rereading the paper, which may help you remember things you had forgotten. This would leave just under 40 minutes per question. Time yourself when you practise questions from this book and learn to work to such time limits.

A good way to select which questions to do is, first of all, to cross out all those you definitely do not want to do and then assess which of the others you might be able to do best. Do this by jotting down a very brief outline or plan for each. This is a skill you can practise and it ensures that you have read the whole question, otherwise you might answer part (a) and then discover that you could not do part (b). It also ensures that you have not missed key words in the stress of the moment.

The next step is to decide which question to do first. Some people like to do their best question first, others feel they can leave this to last because they know it so well they can just reel it off in a shorter time. This again is something you can consider when practising your answers.

If you find you have time at the end of the examination, you might be tempted to answer a further question. In this case the examiner will mark all the questions you have answered and give zero to the one which is least good. However, this is a poor examination strategy. You will gain more marks by rereading what you have already written to jog your memory.

Examiners do not penalize poor handwriting. However, clear handwriting makes the task easier, creating a more favourable impression and a halo effect. If you know your writing is poor, this is a skill you should be practising. Remember, you also gain marks for spelling, punctuation and grammar.

Understanding the question

Everyone says 'read the question carefully' and 'make sure you answer the question set'. Candidates often lose many marks by presenting prepared answers to a different question than the one set. Make sure you do read all the words in the question and that you adapt your answer to the actual question.

You could try the 'machine gun approach': just write everything you know and let the examiner sort out what is relevant. This is unlikely to result in many marks because of lack of selectivity and irrelevance (look at the mark schemes on pp 5–6). It is better to spend your time analysing what the question requires and to do this you must know how to read an examination question:

- **Identify the question parameters**. If the rubric asks you to 'discuss **two** theories ...' then you should cover two theories. If you write about more than two theories, the examiner will only credit the two best covered. Your third theory might be creditworthy *if* it was used to evaluate the others but this needs to be *explicitly* stated.

- **Identify limiting words**. For example, if the question asks you to 'Discuss studies of human attachment' you will get no credit for studies of non-human animals unless these are made explicitly relevant.

- **Familiarize yourself with the meaning of key command words**. Candidates frequently misinterpret terms, especially 'outline', 'assess', 'discuss' and 'research'. The glossary on pp 3–4, adapted from an AEB document, should help you.

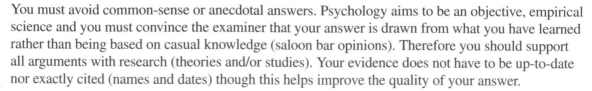

You must avoid common-sense or anecdotal answers. Psychology aims to be an objective, empirical science and you must convince the examiner that your answer is drawn from what you have learned rather than being based on casual knowledge (saloon bar opinions). Therefore you should support all arguments with research (theories and/or studies). Your evidence does not have to be up-to-date nor exactly cited (names and dates) though this helps improve the quality of your answer.

You should state the obvious; what might *seem* obvious to you might not be and the examiner cannot assume that you know information which is not there. On the other hand, you may lose valuable time by describing basic material which is not entirely relevant, such as providing historical context or details of experimental methods.

There are two routes to a good answer: depth or breadth. You could present a few studies/theories but in considerable detail (depth); or you could present a number of studies/theories but, because of time constraints, this will have to be somewhat superficial (breadth). Both can gain high marks as examiners will be aware of the trade-off between the two.

You should be critical. Get into the habit of following every piece of empirical evidence or argument with phrases such as 'This has been criticized by ...', 'An alternative view is ...' or 'This has the advantage of ...'. A few such comments might make a considerable difference to your mark. Theories can be criticized in terms of their quality, coherence, comprehensiveness, alternatives, biases, falsifiability and ability to generate empirical research. Empirical evidence can be criticized in terms of its purpose, participants, apparatus, nature of experimental (or other) procedures, sampling or research biases, findings and conclusions.

Remember that marking is positive; the examiner will credit what is there and not subtract marks for mistakes or for material which is missing.

Also remember that the examiner is looking for ways to discriminate between candidates. An examination would be of little use if all the candidates got the same mark. Therefore it is important that the question separates the weak from the strong candidate. Use the examiner's tips in this book to help you identify how to present a strong answer.

Key command words

Terms which indicate description (AEB calls this Skill A)	
consider	Demonstrate knowledge and understanding of the topic area.
define	Explain what is meant by a particular term or concept.
describe	Present evidence of your knowledge.
examine	Present a detailed, descriptive consideration.
explain	Convey your understanding, coherently and intelligibly.
outline/state	Give a summary description in brief form.

Terms which indicate evaluation (AEB calls this Skill B)	
(critically) analyse	Demonstrate understanding through consideration of the elements of the topic area.
(critically) assess	Make an informed judgement about how good or effective something is, based on an awareness of the strengths and limitations of the information and argument presented.
criticize	Critically evaluate the strengths and weaknesses of the topic area.
(critically) evaluate	Make an informed judgement regarding the value of the topic area, based on systematic analysis.
justify	Consider the grounds for a decision, e.g. by offering a supportive consideration of the logic behind a particular interpretation.

Both Skill A and B terms	
compare/ contrast	Consider similarities and/or differences between the stipulated topic areas.
critically consider	More than just 'consider' (above), to also show an awareness of the strengths and limitations of the material presented.
distinguish between	Demonstrate understanding of the differences between the topic areas; may be achieved at both the level of description and critical contrast.
discuss	Both describe and evaluate by reference to different or contrasting points of view. This may be done sequentially or concurrently. Questions may instruct the candidate to discuss with reference to particular criteria, for example by the use of the phrase 'in terms of'.

Letts
Q&A

Other terms

applications	Actual or possible ways of using psychological knowledge in an applied/practical setting.
concept	An idea or group of ideas, often the basic unit of a model or theory.
evidence	Material (empirical or theoretical) which may be used in support of an argument or theory.
findings	The outcome or product of research.
insights	Perceptions which increase understanding or lead to a new conceptual framework.
methods	Different ways in which empirical research may be carried out.
model	Often used synonymously with 'theory' (see below) but, strictly, less complex.
research	The process of gaining knowledge and understanding through theory, examination, or empirical data collection.
studies	Empirical investigations providing evidence which, through reference to investigator's name and/or details of investigation/outcome, should be recognizable to the examiner.
theory	A (usually) complex set of interrelated ideas/assumptions/principles.

Organizing your answer

An introduction is not necessary in an examination answer but can be a useful way of setting out your essay plan. Do not waste time on historical or background detail. You should paraphrase the question and identify what you will be covering. This is especially important when a quotation has been used in the question; marks are lost if the quotation is not addressed. If the question seems ambiguous, state your understanding of it.

It helps to flag key points. You can enumerate the arguments you present (first, second, third and so on) and you might underline the names of research authors and/or key concepts and theories. It might be best to do the underlining after writing the essay, which would have the added advantage of encouraging you to read through what you have written.

Ideally your answer should be a structured argument rather than a shopping list of loosely related facts.

A conclusion can be a useful means of referring back to the original question and making some final evaluatory remarks on the basis of the arguments you have presented. The point of the conclusion is to state clearly your critical grasp of the topic. Do not waste time with a trite conclusion.

TYPES OF QUESTION

A- and AS-level psychology examinations use a variety of question styles:

- Compulsory short-answer questions: AEB uses these on the Research Methods section of the syllabus, sometimes with a stimulus introduction. Both NEAB and OCSEB include compulsory short-answer questions testing the whole syllabus.

- Stimulus question format: this is popular with NEAB and OCSEB and examples can be found in Unit 9. AEB often uses quotations as a form of stimulus.

- Essay questions: these are either one sentence or divided into two or three parts. When questions are broken down into parts this is intended to help the candidate present a full and critical answer.

MARKING SCHEMES

In Psychology there is no accepted body of knowledge; the corpus is constantly changing as new research is published and social attitudes alter the perspectives that psychologists take. This is reflected in examination mark schemes which have no 'right' answers, only criteria for evaluation. You are examined on how you use your knowledge as well as what you know.

The examiner reads each examination answer carefully and then decides which band or level best describes the answer. Each examination board sets out slightly different criteria but the broad skill areas are:

- Description (AEB calls this the Skill A cluster): your answer should communicate knowledge and understanding of psychological concepts, theories, evidence and applications. You can also demonstrate Skill A through the accuracy, detail and coherence of your answer.

- Analysis and evaluation (AEB calls this the Skill B cluster): you should display critical awareness of your knowledge. This can be demonstrated by noting positive and negative features of the concepts, theories, evidence and applications you mention. You might comment on methodology and usefulness. Skill B can also be demonstrated by drawing on material from across the syllabus (eclecticism) and commenting on individual, social and cultural diversity. Selectivity, coherent elaboration and the effective use of material are also Skill B features.

- Quality of language: spelling, punctuation, grammar and the expression of ideas account for 5% of your total mark.

- Research skills: which are partly assessed in specific parts of the written papers and also in your coursework.

The AEB mark scheme

Skill A	Marks	Psychological content	Accuracy	Detail	Construction	Breadth and/or depth
Band 1 bottom	0-2	Just discernible	Muddled and incomplete	Weak	May be wholly or mainly irrelevant	
Band 1 top	3-4	Basic, rudimentary	Sometimes flawed	Weak	Sometimes focused on the question	
Band 2 bottom	5-6	Limited	Generally accurate	Lacking in detail	Reasonably constructed	Some evidence
Band 2 top	7-8	Appropriate but limited	Accurate	Reasonably detailed	Reasonably constructed	Increasing evidence
Band 3 bottom	9-10	Appropriate but slightly limited	Accurate	Well detailed	Coherent	Balance not always achieved
Band 3 top	11-12	Appropriate	Accurate	Well detailed	Coherent	Substantial evidence and good balance
Skill B		**Commentary**	**Analysis and evaluation**		**Use of material**	**Elaboration**
Band 1 bottom	0-2		Weak, muddled and incomplete		Mainly irrelevant answer, psychological content just discernible	
Band 1 top	3-4	Superficial	Rudimentary		Restricted nature	Minimal interpretation
Band 2 bottom	5-6	Reasonable	Limited		Reasonably effective	Some evidence
Band 2 top	7-8	Reasonable	Appropriate but slightly limited		Effective manner	Evidence of coherent elaboration
Band 3 bottom	9-10	Informed	Appropriate		Effective manner	Coherent elaboration
Band 3 top	11-12	Informed	Thorough		Highly effective manner	Coherently elaborated

The NEAB mark scheme

Poor answers	1–5 marks	Very brief or muddled answer. Psychological content discernible but description weak and little understanding. May be largely irrelevant to the question.
Weak–Average	6–10 marks	Appropriate description of psychological theories and evidence, generally accurate but limited and not well detailed. Attempts to answer the question. May be some limited analysis and evaluation.
Average–Good	11–15 marks	Appropriate psychological evidence presented which is accurate and well detailed showing knowledge and understanding. For marks at the top of the band there must be some discussion of the issues raised, i.e. evaluation, analysis or application. Answers will show increasing organization in structure and coherence.
Excellent	16–20 marks	Answers in this band will show a sound grasp of the important issues raised by the question. They will present selected, relevant material in a coherent, organized manner. Such material will be accurate and well detailed. Appropriate analysis and evaluation will also be present as may illustrations and applications of psychological concepts and theories.

The OCSEB mark scheme for specialist choice examination questions

The specialist choice questions are always presented in the same three parts:

		SKILL LEVEL 1		SKILL LEVEL 2
Part (a)	Knowledge: psychological terminology, concepts, theories.	Some appropriate. (1 mark)		Appropriate. (2 marks)
	Knowledge: psychological/ theoretical evidence.	Some. (1 mark)		Accurately described. (2 marks)
Total 8 marks	Understanding.	Some. (1 mark)	Meaning identified. (2 marks)	Clear and detailed, use of wider context. (3 or 4 marks)
Part (b)	Evaluation.	Only one criterion. (1 mark)	Several criteria, limited in scope/detail. (2 marks)	Number of criteria, wide ranging and detailed. (3 or 4 marks)
	Research skills methodology.	Some appropriate limitations. (1 mark)		Awareness of strengths and weaknesses. (2 marks)
Total 10 marks	Analysis: key points identified.	Reasonable. (1 mark)	Limited attempt to draw out relationship. (2 marks)	Valid generalizations, answer wide ranging and detailed. (3 or 4 marks)
Part (c) Total	Knowledge: evidence.	Anecdotal. (1 mark)	Limited in scope and detail. (2 marks)	Accurate, wide ranging and detailed. (3 or 4 marks)
6 marks	Application of appropriate evidence.	Reasonable. (1 mark)		Effective. (2 marks)

Social cognition

❶ Social influences upon perception: you should cover theories and research related to how social factors influence the way we perceive others and the world generally. Examples include *cultural identity*, *social identity theory* (**Tajfel**) and *social representations* (or *schema*).

❷ Attribution theory: relevant theories include the *correspondent inference theory* (**Jones and Davis**) and **Kelley's** theory of *causal schemata*. You should be familiar with various errors and biases in the attribution process, such as the *fundamental attribution error* and the *self-serving bias*.

❸ Prejudice and discrimination: it is necessary to be able to account for the origins and maintenance of prejudice and discrimination. Explanations include the *prejudiced personality* (**Adorno**, a social learning approach), the *scapegoat theory* (**Weatherly**, a psychodynamic approach), *social* and *cultural stereotypes* (a cognitive-informational approach), *conformity* (an interpersonal approach), and *realistic conflict* and *social identity theory* (e.g. **Tajfel**, intergroup approaches). You should also have a critical understanding of the methods of reducing prejudice and discrimination, for example, through increased social contact, co-operation, positive images and legislation.

Social relationships

❶ Theories of interpersonal relationships: these include the *reinforcement-affect model* (**Byrne**), *balance theory* (**Newcombe**), *equity theory* (**Walster** *et al.*), *social exchange theory* (**Thibaut and Kelley**) and *matched self-disclosure* (**Duck**). A theory may be any structured body of facts and therefore you could present the factors important in relationship formation (see below) as a theory.

❷ Formation, maintenance and dissolution of relationships: you should be familiar with explanations and research evidence for these stages of interpersonal relationships. Formation can be understood in terms of factors such as *physical attraction, proximity, reciprocity, similarity* and *competence*. Maintenance and dissolution can be explained by theories of interpersonal relationships.

❸ Components of interpersonal relationships: you should be able to discuss factors which explain the dynamics of relationships, such as goals, conflicts, rules, power and roles. You should consider individual, social and cultural variations in the nature of relationships.

❹ Effects of interpersonal relationships: the success or failure of relationships affects, for example, happiness and mental health.

Social influence

❶ Conformity, obedience and independent behaviour: you should have a critical knowledge of research relating to conformity (e.g. **Sherif**, **Asch** and **Crutchfield**) and research on obedience (e.g. **Milgram**, **Zimbardo** and **Hofling**). Related topics include *compliance, norm formation, non-conformity* (*independent behaviour*), and the effects of *group* and *cultural pressures*. You might also consider: *social facilitation, groupthink* and the *bystander effect*.

❷ Social power (leadership and followership): the emergence and effectiveness of leaders can be explained in terms of personality (*trait theories*), situation, leadership skills, behavioural style (**Lewin** *et al.*) and an interaction between situation and style, for instance *contingency theory* (**Fiedler**) or *normative theory* (**Vroom and Yetton**). You should be familiar with theories and research relating to these explanations. Other issues which should be considered include: status, power and the behaviour of followers (see conformity and obedience).

REVISION SUMMARY

❸ **Collective behaviour**: crowd behaviour can be explained by factors such as *bystander arousal (density-intensity hypothesis), apathy, deindividuation* and *social contagion*. You should be able to distinguish between crowds and *mobs*, and crowds and *crowding*.

Prosocial and antisocial behaviour

❶ **Altruism and bystander behaviour**: you should be able to distinguish between altruism and *helping behaviour*, and be able to discuss theories and research related to *bystander behaviour*, for example, how characteristics of the situation, the victim, and the bystander, all contribute to helping behaviour. You should be familiar with the concepts of *pluralistic ignorance, diffusion of responsibility, evaluation apprehension* and *intervention costs*. You should consider individual, social and cultural diversity in prosocial behaviour.

❷ **Theories of aggression**: aggression can be explained from various perspectives: *biological* (hormones and heredity), *ethological* (**Lorenz**), *social learning* (the effects of families and of the media), *motivational* (the *arousal-aggression hypothesis*) and *psychodynamic* (**Freud**). You should consider individual, social and cultural diversity in antisocial behaviour.

❸ **Reduction and control of aggression**: ideas include: unlearning, removing cues, teaching non-aggressive skills, channelling aggression (*catharsis*), ritualization, psychosurgery and use of chemicals (drugs). The different methods can be related to the different theories of aggression.

❹ **Media influences**: you should be familiar with theories and research related to how the media may influence prosocial and antisocial behaviour, how the media promotes social stereotypes and how we might control these influences (censorship and *counter-stereotyping*). You should have a critical understanding of the arguments relating to the effects of violence on television, for example, direct effects (such as *imitation*), indirect effects (*desensitization, disinhibition* and *arousal*), the exaggeration of pre-existing tendencies, and TV violence as a form of *catharsis*.

Additional points for other candidates
NEAB

- The **Social Psychology module** includes: prejudice (termed 'conflict'), conformity, obedience, leadership and attribution theory. **Plus**: attitudes (measurement, formation and change), groups (group polarization, social facilitation, group decision making), impression formation (perception of others and self-perception), and applications (eyewitness testimony and juries).

- The **Contemporary Topics module** (see Unit 9) includes: interpersonal relationships and group processes (including leadership). **Plus**: intimate relationships (love and marriage, sex and sexual relationships and problems in relationships).

OCSEB

- The **Social Interaction section** (compulsory) includes: conformity, obedience and social relationships (affiliation). **Plus**: the influence of social roles on behaviour, and the social and cultural context of research.

- The **Social Cognition section** (compulsory) includes: attribution theory, prejudice and discrimination. **Plus**: theories of attitude change.

- The **Psychology and the Environment specialist choice** (see Unit 9) includes: collective and bystander behaviour.

- The **Psychology and Organizations specialist choice** (see Unit 9) includes: inter- and intragroup behaviour, and leadership style.

If you need to revise this subject more thoroughly, see the relevant topics in the *Letts* A-level *Psychology Study Guide*.

- The **Psychology and Sport specialist choice** (see Unit 9) includes: audience effects, leadership, group processes, theories of aggression and the effects of attribution.

1 (a)   What do psychologists mean by the terms *prejudice* and *discrimination*?   (4)

 (b) Describe and evaluate **one** psychological study of prejudice reduction **or** discrimination reduction.   (10)

 (c) Critically consider why many attempts to reduce prejudice or discrimination have failed.   (10)

AEB (specimen)

2 Describe and evaluate **two** psychological theories of interpersonal relationships.   (24)

3 Critically consider social-psychological research into factors associated with independence.   (24)

AEB (specimen)

4 Critically consider the view that the media might contribute to the development of aggressive behaviour.   (24)

AEB

(There is a further question related to the social psychology syllabus in Unit 9, on crowd and bystander behaviour.)

2 *Comparative psychology*

Evolutionary determinants of behaviour

❶ **Evolutionary concepts**: the basic principles of evolution are *natural selection* and *survival of the fittest* (**Darwin**). You should understand the concepts of *adaptedness*, *ecological niche* and *fitness*, as well as *genotype* and *phenotype* (**Mendelian genetics**), *group selection* (**Wynne-Edwards**), *inclusive fitness* (**Hamilton**) and *kin selection* (**Wilson**). There are other derived concepts such as *phylogeny* and *ontogeny*, *neoteny* (**Gould**), *canalization* (**Waddington**), *coevolution*, *evolutionarily stable strategies* (*ESS*), and *cost functions* (decrements and increments in fitness). Various ethological concepts should also be familiar, such as *sign stimuli*, *fixed action patterns*, *releasers* and *instinct*.

❷ **Competition for resources**: the term 'resources' refers to such things as food, mates and nesting sites. Limited availability means that individuals must find means of managing these resources, for example, the use of *territories*, *dominance hierarchies*, *ritualized fighting*, *intraspecies exploitation* (selfish behaviour as opposed to altruism) and *resource defence*.

❸ **Interspecies relationships**: you should understand how certain interspecies relationships affect the evolution of behaviour patterns in both species, for example, *predator–prey* and *symbiotic* relationships. Behavioural outcomes include the use of honest and dishonest signals (e.g. *manipulation theory* and *mimicry*), social grouping (e.g. fish schooling as a means of defence) and the '*arms race*' (**Dawkins** and **Krebs**).

Reproductive strategies

❶ **Sexual selection**: in certain species selection may be determined by an existing dominance hierarchy or other social structure, whereas solitary animals must use signals to locate mates. Mate selection is achieved through courtship rituals and sexual attraction (such as *bizarre characteristics*). There are different male (*intrasexual*) and female (*intersexual*) strategies.

❷ **Parental investment**: factors which may influence the degree of investment include the number of offspring, maturity at birth, the means of fertilization, and the kind of pair bonding (*monogamy*, *polygamy* or *polyandry*). Theoretical accounts have been offered by **Ridley** (*paternity certainty hypothesis*), **Dawkins** and **Carlisle** (*order of gamete release hypothesis*) and **Williams** (*association hypothesis*).

❸ **Social organization**: you should understand how the mating strategies of a species influence its social organization.

❹ **Parent–offspring conflict**: you should be able to present evolutionary arguments of parent–offspring conflict, discussing the gains and costs to both.

Kinship and social behaviour

❶ **Apparent altruism**: you should be critically familiar with examples of, and genetic explanations for, apparent altruism. This involves understanding *kin selection* (**Hamilton** and **Wilson**) and the concept of the *selfish gene* (**Dawkins**). You should be aware that altruism benefits a particular gene line and not a species (i.e. not *group selection*). You should also consider *reciprocal* and *manipulated altruism* (the *Green Beard effect*).

❷ **Sociality in non-human animals**: you should be familiar with the kinds of social relations which exist between non-human animals including social co-operation as a means of defence and attack in predator–prey relationships. A critical appreciation of the advantages and disadvantages might include an understanding of dominance hierarchies (*pecking order*, *matriline groups*), cultural inheritance and solitary living.

❸ **Imprinting and bonding**: you should be familiar with the consequences of imprinting (*precocial* species) and *bonding* (*altricial* species), and related concepts such as *critical* and *sensitive periods*, *irreversibility*, the *following response*, and *filial* and *sexual imprinting*. You should be able to assess the usefulness and biological significance of these concepts and the extent to which imprinting and bonding are distinct from other forms of learning.

❹ **Signalling systems in non-human animals**: you should have a critical understanding of the various channels for communication: vision, audition, olfaction, gustation, touch (pressure and grooming), and electrical and magnetic sensitivity. You should consider the signalling systems of a number of different species, including some more advanced ones like those of marine mammals and apes, as well as birdsong, danger signals in rabbits, and scent trails in ants. An analysis of signalling can be in terms of *encoding*, *transmission*, *detection* and *decoding* between members of the same or different non-human species, *verbal* and *non-verbal* signals, *honest* and *dishonest* signals, and the origins of signals (e.g. *intention movements*, *displacement*, *autonomic displays*).

Behaviour analysis

❶ **Classical and operant conditioning**: you should have a critical appreciation of the theories of classical (**Pavlov**) and operant conditioning (**Thorndike** and **Skinner**). Application of the theory can be used as a means of evaluation. You might look at how conditioning theory can be applied, for example, in teaching, therapy, advertising and biofeedback.

❷ **Learning in the natural environment**: you should be able to use explanations of learning in the natural environment to understand *foraging* and *homing* behaviour. Possible explanations include *habituation*, *sensitization*, *associative learning* (not classical conditioning), *imprinting* and *perceptual learning*. Laboratory studies of learning are relevant only where they shed light on natural behaviour.

❸ **Animal language**: psychological research into animal language includes attempts to teach human language to non-human animals (e.g. **Gardner and Gardner**, **Terrace**, **Premack**, **Savage-Rumbaugh**, **Pepperberg**) and to consider instances of natural animal language, such as in bees (**von Frisch**), chimpanzees (**Menzel**), and cetaceans. You should be able to distinguish between signalling and language; **Hockett's** design features of language will be helpful.

❹ **Evolutionary explanations of human behaviour**: you should have a critical understanding of the extent to which *human* behaviour can be explained in terms of evolutionary concepts. Candidates might apply such concepts to explanations of sleep, sexual behaviour, altruism and language.

Additional points for other candidates

NEAB

- The **Perspectives in Psychology module** (compulsory) includes: genetic (evolutionary) explanations of behaviour, and classical and operant conditioning.

- The **Cognitive Psychology and Its Applications module** includes: a comparison of human language and communication systems in other animals.

OCSEB

- The **Comparative Psychology section** (compulsory) includes: evolutionary concepts, comparison between communication and language, and evolutionary explanations of human behaviour. **Plus**: ethological concepts and the relevance of animal research (see Unit 7).

If you need to revise this subject more thoroughly, see the relevant topics in the *Letts* A-level *Psychology Study Guide*.

2 Comparative psychology

• The **Psychology and Sport specialist choice** (see Unit 9) includes: learning (conditioning).

1 Describe and critically assess the effects of predator–prey relationships on the evolution of behaviour patterns. (24)

2 (a) Describe two different approaches to the differential investments of males and females in the rearing of the young. (6)

(b) Discuss a psychological explanation for differential investments of males and females in the rearing of the young. (18)

AEB (specimen)

3 'Darwinians believe that natural selection is the only cause of adaptation. Natural selection cannot (it seems) cause altruism. But altruism exists. That is the paradox.' (Ridley, 1986)

With reference to the above quote, discuss the role of apparent altruism in the behaviour of non-human animals. (24)

AEB

4 (a) Explain what psychologists mean by the terms language and communication. (10)

(b) Describe and evaluate any **one** comparative study of communication in non-human animals. (14)

AEB

Basic neural and hormonal processes and their influence on behaviour

❶ **The central and autonomic nervous systems (CNS and ANS) and the endocrine system**: you should be able to describe the three systems in terms of their organization, structure and function, and be aware of the interactions between them.

❷ **Influences on physiological and behavioural functions**: you should be aware of how the CNS, ANS and endocrine system influence physiological and behavioural functions, including *homeostasis* in relation to hunger, thirst, temperature and sex.

❸ **Neural transmission**: you should understand *neuronal* and *synaptic* activity, and be able to suggest how such processes might relate to behaviour, such as experience of pain, effects of drugs, or in relation to schizophrenia. Key concepts include *chemical transmitters*, *excitation* and *inhibition*, and the conditional nature of messages.

❹ **Drugs and behaviour**: you should be familiar with research into the effects of various drugs on behaviour, for instance the effects of depressants, anti-depressants, major tranquillizers, stimulants, pain killers, narcotics and hallucinogens on different kinds of behaviour, such as aggression, sexual behaviour and sensorimotor co-ordination.

Cortical functions

❶ **Investigation of cortical activity**: you should have a critical appreciation of the methods and techniques used to investigate cortical functioning, for example, techniques with no side effects (*EEG*, *X-ray tomography*, testing *neurospinal fluid*), techniques using deliberate damage (*ablation*, *lesions*, *implanted electrodes*) and brain injury or illness (accidents, operations, *split brain studies*, post-mortem examinations).

❷ **Localization of function in the brain**: you should consider both human and non-human research into the localization of sensory processes (touch, hearing, vision), motor processes, language, memory and emotion. You should be able to distinguish between *lateralization*, *specialization* and *localization*.

❸ **Neurophysiological basis of visual perception**: you should know how the structures of the visual system relate to both visual sensation and visual perception. This includes the eye, *retina*, *lateral geniculate body* and *visual cortex* (e.g. **Hubel and Wiesel**). You might consider how colour, movement, shape and depth are perceived at both retinal and cortical levels.

Awareness

❶ **Bodily rhythms**: this covers any aspect of behaviour which exhibits periodicity. There are diurnal or *circadian* rhythms (such as sleep/waking), *ultradian* rhythms which are shorter than a day (e.g. sleep and dream stages, heart beat) and *infradian* rhythms lasting longer than a day (e.g. menstrual cycle, seasonal mating, migration). Such rhythms may be regular or irregular, and can be understood in terms of physiological and psychological factors, such as external influences (e.g. light, smell, temperature) and internal mechanisms (*suprachiasmatic nucleus*, *biological clock*, influence of hormones). You should also be aware of the applications of such research, for example, mental health (*seasonal affective disorder*), shift work and jet lag.

❷ **States of awareness**: you should be familiar with physiological and psychological explanations of states of awareness, including sleep and dream states, levels of consciousness and their neuroanatomical/neurophysiological correlates. Different levels of awareness can be related to bodily rhythms.

❸ **Theories of sleep**: the function of sleep has been explained by the *repair and restoration theory* (**Oswald**), *neurochemical models* (**Jouvet**), *evolutionary theory* (**Meddis**) and *hibernation theory*. You should be familiar with relevant research, such as the effects of sleep deprivation (and the *REM rebound*), activity, age and observations of sleep patterns in different species. You should also be aware of theories of dreams, such as the *activation–synthesis model* (**McCarley**), *consolidation theory* (**Ornstein**), *cognitive restoration* (**Evans**) and *emotional catharsis* (**Freud**).

❹ **Hypnotic states**: you should be familiar with theories and research studies into the phenomenon of hypnosis. Explanations include *neo-dissociation theory*, the *placebo effect*, and relaxation. You should consider individual differences, susceptibility, self-hypnosis, posthypnotic amnesia, age regression, reduced sensitivity, hallucinations and applications of hypnosis to, for example, medicine.

Motivation, emotion and stress

❶ **Motivation**: you should have a critical knowledge of motivation research related to eating, drinking, sex, avoidance of pain and learning. You should distinguish between human and non-human motives, homeostatic and non-homeostatic motives, and internal (physiological or psychological) and external (social context and learning) factors. Theoretical accounts include physiological ones, such as *homeostatic drive theory* (**Cannon**), *drive-reduction theory* (**Hull**) and *arousal theory*, and non-physiological (psychological) models, such as *instinct* (**James**), *hydraulic model* (ethological), cognitive accounts (e.g. **Tolman, McClelland, White**), humanistic approaches (**Maslow, Rogers**) and *psychoanalytic theory* (**Freud**). You should be familiar with relevant brain structures, chiefly the *limbic system* and *hypothalamus*.

❷ **Emotion**: You should understand both physiological and non-physiological explanations of emotion, namely the **James-Lange** *theory*, **Cannon-Bard** *theory*, *cognitive labelling theory* (**Schachter**), and *cognitive appraisal theory* (**Smith and Ellsworth**). You should also be familiar with related empirical research and the brain structures associated with emotion, namely the *limbic system*.

❸ **Stress**: You should have a critical understanding of theories and research relating to sources of stress (life and daily events, environmental and work stimuli, conflict, traumatic events), responses to stress (physiological/psychological, long/short-term, positive/negative – *eustress* and *distress*), individual differences (*type A personality*, hardiness, farsightedness), situational factors (predictability, *locus of control*, social support), and methods of coping. Coping strategies may be emotion- or problem-focused: behavioural (*relaxation, systematic desensitization, modelling*), cognitive (*restructuring, rational emotive therapy*) or physiological methods (*biofeedback, anxiolytic drugs*). You should understand the relationship between stress and illness (e.g. cancer, allergies, and gastrointestinal and cardiovascular disorders), and relevant research (e.g. **Brady**, **Selye** (*GAS*), **Holmes and Rahe**, **Friedman and Rosenman**).

Additional points for other candidates
NEAB

- The **Perspectives in Psychology module** (compulsory) includes: neuronal and hormonal explanations of behaviour, and localization in the brain.

- The **Health Psychology module** (see Unit 9) includes: stress and illness.

- The **Psychology in Education module** (see Unit 9) includes: the effects of stress on performance.

If you need to revise this subject more thoroughly, see the relevant topics in the *Letts* **A-level** *Psychology Study Guide.*

OCSEB

- The **Physiological Psychology section** (compulsory) includes: emotion, sleep, and basic neural processes. **Plus**: evaluation of the physiological approach (see Unit 7).

- The **Psychology and Health specialist choice** (see Unit 9) includes: stress.

- The **Psychology and the Environment specialist choice** (see Unit 9) includes: factors known to create environmental stress.

- The **Psychology and Sport specialist choice** (see Unit 9) includes: motivation.

REVISION SUMMARY

QUESTIONS

1 (a) Describe the structure and function of **either** the autonomic nervous system **or** the endocrine system. (12)

   (b) Assess the effects that the system you have described has been shown to have on physiological and behavioural functions. (12)

   AEB (specimen)

2 Discuss some of the findings of research into localization of function in the human cerebral cortex. (24)

   AEB

3 Compare and contrast any **two** theories of sleep. (24)

   AEB

4 'For the past 100 years scientists have known that the bodily changes that accompany emotional arousal are commanded by the brain. But how the brain functions to produce these changes and how the changes relate to emotions remain a matter of controversy.'

   Discuss this statement in relation to the role of physiological factors in emotion. (24)

   AEB

4 *Atypical development and abnormal behaviour*

Atypical development

❶ **Learning difficulties**: you should be familiar with the causes of and problems associated with learning difficulties. Causes include *mental retardation*, *dyslexia* or other *specific learning disabilities*. You should consider both psychological and neurological (within-child) explanations, environmental influences, interactive perspectives, advantages and disadvantages of special education, the involvement of educational psychologists, *statements*, and the problem of *labelling*.

❷ **Physical and sensory handicaps**: you should study physical handicaps (e.g. *Down's syndrome*, *cerebral palsy*, *spina bifida*, *diabetes*) and sensory handicaps (e.g. *visual* and *hearing impairment*). You should have a critical understanding of the primary and secondary effects of such handicaps and the problems of coping with them.

❸ **Emotional disturbances and behavioural problems**: you should be familiar with the causes and effects of emotional and behavioural problems in childhood and adolescence, for example, *attention-deficit hyperactivity disorder*, *autism* and *developmental dyslexia*. You might also consider eating problems (*anorexia* and *bulimia*), *conduct disorder*, *childhood schizophrenia* and *depression*.

Conceptions and models of abnormality

❶ **Definitions and classifications of normal and abnormal behaviours**: the question of defining (ab)normality may be approached in terms of statistical frequency, social deviation, mental healthiness (**Jahoda**), and the *medical model*. Other explanations include the *existential model* (**Laing**), personal distress (**Atkinson** *et al.*) and maladaptiveness (**Rosenhan and Seligman**). Notable critics include **Szasz**, **Heather**, **Rosenhan** and **Foucault**. You should be aware of alternative approaches to the classification of abnormality, including the DSM and ICD schemes. A critical appreciation of the associated practical and ethical problems will include issues such as reliability of diagnosis (inter- and intra-observer), validity (descriptive, i.e. symptoms, and predictive, i.e. prognosis), cultural and social influences on diagnosis, the problems of *labelling* and *stereotyping*, the sick role, demand characteristics of the consultation process, and rights and responsibilities of patients and clinicians. You should also consider the relationship between classification and treatment.

❷ **Alternative paradigms in abnormal psychology**: you should be aware of the assumptions underlying the *medical*, *behavioural*, *cognitive*, *humanistic* and *psychodynamic* models. It is also important to consider the ethical and therapeutic implications of each model.

❸ **Cultural and subcultural differences**: there are important cultural and subcultural differences in defining abnormality, including biases in relation to diagnosis and classification. You should also consider racism and sexism.

Psychopathology

Explanations of abnormalities: your study should include descriptions of the following: *schizophrenia* (especially the *diathesis-stress model*), depression or *affective disorders*, *anxiety disorders* (e.g. *phobias* and *post-traumatic stress*) and *eating disorders*. You should be acquainted with alternative explanations for all of these disorders, especially the relative contributions of biological (genetic, neurochemical or neuroanatomical) and environmental (social and psychological) factors.

Therapeutic approaches

❶ **Types of therapies and treatments**: you should include behaviour therapies (e.g. *aversion therapy*, *systematic desensitization*, *flooding*, *token economy*), cognitive therapies *(modelling,* **Kelly's** *personal construct therapy)*, cognitive-behavioural therapies (e.g. **Ellis'** *rational emotive therapy*), humanistic therapies (e.g. **Roger's** *counselling*), psychodynamic therapies (**Freud** and neo-Freudians such as **Jung** and **Adler**, *free association, rich interpretation, dream analysis, transference*) and somatic approaches (*ECT, psychosurgery, drug therapies*). You should be critically aware of outcome measures used to assess the appropriateness and effectiveness of treatments, and problems related to such assessments, such as reliability and validity, lack of control groups, spontaneous remission, client/therapist interaction, disorder/therapy interaction, expectation and placebo effects, lack of long-term follow-up evidence, definitions of a cure and patient/client assessment. You should also consider the relationship between diagnosis and therapy, as well as relevant political and social issues. Questions about which therapy to choose involve issues such as the effectiveness of certain therapies in relation to specific illnesses and/or types of client, the client's desire and/or ability to be actively involved, side effects and client/family choice.

❷ **Ethical issues**: you should be aware of the ethical issues involved in therapy and intervention, for example, patient's rights (informed consent and confidentiality), side effects of treatments, dehumanization, *labelling* and the choice of goals. You might also consider the problem in terms of a cost–benefit analysis and consider the outlook for patients who receive no treatment or alternative treatments.

Additional points for other candidates

NEAB

- The **Perspectives in Psychology module** (compulsory) includes: psychodynamic (Freud and post-Freudian, Erikson) and humanistic (Rogers and Maslow) approaches.

- The **Psychology of Atypical Behaviour module** includes: definition and classification of normality and abnormality, alternative paradigms, psychopathology (including also obsessive-compulsive behaviour and organic disorders), therapeutic approaches and ethics. **Plus**: research methods in atypical psychology.

- The **Health Psychology module** (see Unit 9) includes: eating disorders.

- The **Psychology in Education module** (see Unit 9) includes: learning difficulties, labelling in education and dyslexia.

OCSEB

- The **Cognitive Psychology section** (compulsory) includes: autism.

- The **Abnormal Psychology section** (compulsory) includes: definitions and classifications of normal and abnormal behaviours, alternative paradigms and psychopathology. **Plus**: evaluation of research methods.

- The **Psychology and Education specialist choice** (see Unit 9) includes: behaviour problems in school.

If you need to revise this subject more thoroughly, see the relevant topics in the *Letts* A-level *Psychology Study Guide*.

1 Describe some of the psychological effects of physical and sensory disabilities and evaluate these in terms of child development. (24)

2 Discuss the assumptions which underlie the medical model of abnormality. (24)

3 (a) Outline the main symptoms of schizophrenia. (4)

   (b) Discuss evidence for biological and environmental influences. (16)

   NEAB

4 (a) Describe treatments which are based on the somatic approach to mental illness. (10)

   (b) Discuss the difficulties involved in evaluating the effectiveness of these treatments. (14)

   AEB

Perceptual processes

(Note that the emphasis in this section is on the visual system but you can consider other senses as well.)

❶ Theories of perception: you should be familiar with *top-down* (or *constructivist*) *theories* such as **Gregory's** and *bottom-up* (or *direct*) *models* such as **Gibson's**. Other theories include **Neisser's** *analysis-by-synthesis* and **Marr's** *computational theory of vision*.

❷ Perceptual development: you should know the details of research which supports the *innate* position (e.g. studies of human and animal neonates), and research illustrating the *environmental* view (e.g. readjustment, distortion, deprivation and cross-cultural studies). It is useful to be familiar with the various practical techniques and ethical problems related to such studies.

❸ Perceptual organization: the process of organizing sensory data into meaningful units can be explained by: theories of *pattern recognition* (e.g. templates or **Gestalt** principles), *perceptual constancies* (e.g. shape, movement, colour and depth) and *perceptual set*, a bias created by the situation (e.g. context, ambiguity, language) or the perceiver (e.g. expectation, emotion, motivation, culture). *Illusions*, and the theories used to explain them, are a means of illustrating perceptual organization. You should be aware of individual, social and cultural variations in perceptual organization.

Attention and performance limitations

❶ Focused attention: you should be familiar with the following theories of focused (selective) visual attention and their related empirical evidence: the *filter theory* (**Broadbent**), the *attenuator model* (**Treisman**) and the *late selection model* (**Deutsch and Deutsch**). More recent models offer combined accounts of focused and divided attention (e.g. **Kahneman, Johnston and Heinz**).

❷ Divided attention: you should have a critical appreciation of relevant empirical evidence and theoretical accounts of divided attention, including **Kahneman's** *central capacity model* and **Allport's** *modular approach*.

❸ Automatic processing: you should be aware of the theory and research relevant to automatic processing, such as that of **Posner and Snyder**.

❹ Performance deficits: you should be familiar with theories and research related to deficits, including *action slips* and *dual task limitations*.

Memory

❶ Models of memory: you should be familiar with research concerned with the nature, structure, processes and types of memory. Relevant explanations include the *multistore model* (**Atkinson and Shiffrin**), *working memory* (**Baddeley**), *semantic* and *episodic memory* (**Tulving**), *procedural* and *declarative memory* (**Cohen and Squires**), *levels of processing* (**Craik and Lockhart**) and *reconstructive memory* (**Bartlett**). Evidence for these models is gathered by looking at the effects of such things as position (*serial position effect*), organization, capacity, duration and types of coding (acoustic or semantic).

❷ Organization of memory: there is an overlap between models of memory and the question of how memory is organized. Organization specifically refers to the way that data is stored. Explanations include the use of *categories* (**Mandler**), *hierarchies* (**Collins and Quillan**), *networks* (**McClelland**) or *schema* (**Bartlett**).

❸ **Forgetting**: you should consider two kinds of explanation: failures of *availability* and failures of *accessibility*. Examples of availability include *trace decay*, *displacement*, *interference* and *brain damage*. Accessibility is influenced by a lack of retrieval cues (*cue-dependent forgetting*), by *repression* (motivated forgetting) and by *set* due to the influence, for example, of language or schema.

❹ **Practical applications of memory research**: relevant research and examples include: *face recognition* (photofits), police reconstructions of crime, eye witness testimony, advice for exam revision (*mnemonic techniques*) and memory for medical information.

Language and thought

❶ **Language acquisition**: you should be familiar with the sequence of language acquisition, research findings into the process of language acquisition and with theories of language development, including *learning theory* (**Skinner**), *nativist theory* (**Chomsky**) and *enrichment theory* (**Piaget**).

❷ **Production and comprehension**: theories and research related to the production (e.g. speaking and writing) and the comprehension (e.g. listening and reading) of language should be covered.

❸ **Models of thought**: you should be able to define thinking (e.g. as association, as cognitive restructuring, as adaptation). You should understand the various different ways of thinking: *convergent* and *divergent* (creative) thinking, *cognitive styles*, *reasoning*, *decision making* and *problem solving*. There are various theories of problem-solving, such as *trial-and-error* (**Thorndike**), *insight* (**Köhler**), development of learning *sets* (*functional fixedness*), *lateral* thinking (**deBono**) and *brainstorming*. Various suggestions have been offered to explain the way we represent knowledge, for example, *concepts* (**Collins and Quillan**), *schema* (**Schank and Abelson**), *cognitive maps* (**Tolman**), *modes of thinking* (**Bruner**). You should also consider the problem of thinking about thinking and the techniques used in relevant research, such as introspection, thinking aloud, behavioural observation, measuring reaction times and computer models.

❹ **Relationship between language and thought**: the relationship between language and thought should be understood in the light of theories put forward by **Whorf**, **Piaget** and **Vygotsky**. The difference between linguistic *determinism* and linguistic *relativity* should be appreciated, as well as the view that thought exists independently of language. You should also consider social and cultural variations in language in relation to thought.

If you need to revise this subject more thoroughly, see the relevant topics in the *Letts* A-level *Psychology Study Guide*.

Additional points for other candidates
NEAB

• The **Perspectives in Psychology module** (compulsory) includes: assumptions of the cognitive approach, development of ideas from information processing and computer technology, computer analogies.

• The **Cognitive Psychology and Its Applications module** includes: theories of perception and perceptual organization, focused (selective) and divided attention, memory, language and thought, models of thought. **Plus**: the nature and functions of language in human and non-human animals (see Unit 2); problem-solving and artificial intelligence (weak and strong AI, computer problem-solving techniques).

• The **Child Development module** includes: language acquisition (see Unit 6).

OCSEB

- The **Cognitive Psychology section** (compulsory) includes: models of memory. **Plus**: cultural differences in cognitive performance; autism and the theory of mind.

- The **Psychology and Organizations specialist choice** (see Unit 9) includes: research on decision making.

1 (a) Give a definition of perception. (4)

    (b) Describe any **one** theory or model of perception. (10)

    (c) Evaluate this theory in terms of its explanation of perceptual processes. (10)
AEB

2 Describe and evaluate experimental studies of selective attention. (24)
AEB

3 Discuss the view that there are different types of memory. (24)
AEB

4 Discuss **two or more** theories of the relationship between language and thought. (24)
AEB (specimen)

Letts
Q&A

6 *Developmental psychology*

Early socialization

❶ Sociability and attachments: you should have a critical understanding of theories and research relating to social development in the first years of life, chiefly the development of sociability and attachments. This will include the work of **Bowlby**, **Ainsworth**, **Rutter**, **Schaffer**, and **Clarke and Clarke**. Note that early socialization involves more than maternal care, and that the effects are both short and long term. You should consider the implications of research for child care practices.

❷ Enrichment and deprivation: the effects of enrichment and deprivation should be considered in relation to maternal care, perception and language. Key studies might include Project Headstart, research on hothousing (**Howe**), limited visual experience (**Blakemore and Cooper**, **Held and Hein**, **Banks**), institutionalized children (**Tizard**, **Dennis**, **White and Held**) and isolated children (**Curtiss**, **Dennis**). You should distinguish between the effects of *deprivation* and *privation*.

❸ Social and cultural variations in child rearing: you should be familiar with research into culturally-specific aspects of child-rearing, cross-cultural differences and the effects of such differences, for example, studies by **Fox**, **Ainsworth** and **Mead**.

Cognitive development

❶ Theories of cognitive development: you should have a critical understanding of the theories of **Piaget** and **Vygotsky**, and of the *Information Processing approach* (e.g. **Fischer**). You could also consider the work of **Bruner**. You should be acquainted with the evidence upon which these theories are based.

❷ Practical applications in education: you should be aware of how theories of cognitive development can be applied to educational practices, for example, in designing teaching strategies, such as *discovery learning* versus the use of *expert intervention*, and the concept of *readiness* versus *training*. Education can be interpreted in the broadest sense and not limited to classroom practice, for example, applications in toy manufacture, parenting, advertising and therapeutic practice.

❸ Development of measured intelligence: you should be familiar with issues concerning intelligence test performance, including genetic and environmental influences. The genetic position is supported by twin studies (**Burt**, **Shields**), familial links (**Bouchard and McGue**), and adoption studies (**Skodak and Skeels**, **Horn**). The environmental position is supported by the effects of diet (**Benton**), parental attention (**Zajonc and Markus**), social class (**Sameroff**) and enrichment (**Operation Headstart**). There are certain key arguments, such as the interaction between nature and nurture, the question of polygenetic inheritance and the link between race and intelligence (e.g. **Jensen**, **Bodmer**).

Social development and diversity in development

❶ Moral development: your study should include theoretical accounts of moral (prosocial) development, chiefly *social learning* (**Bandura**, **Mischel**), *psychodynamic* (**Freud**) and *cognitive-developmental* (**Piaget**, **Kohlberg**, **Eisenberg**) *theories*, as well as a critical knowledge of the evidence on which these theories are based. Moral development can be explained in terms of internal processes (e.g. cognitions and maturation) or external influences, such as gender, family (child-rearing style, emotional tone, methods of control, communication patterns, family dynamics), ethnic group and social class, peer group, the school and the media. Finally, you should be aware of different moral orientations (**Gilligan**), moral inconsistency (e.g. **Hartshorne and May**) and cultural variation (e.g. **Nobles**).

2 **Gender development**: you should be aware of definitions related to sex and gender, and theories of gender development: *biological* (**Money**), *social learning* (**Bandura**, **Mischel**), *psychodynamic* (**Freud**), *cognitive-developmental* (**Kohlberg**), and *gender-schema theories* (**Bem**). You should be critically acquainted with the evidence on which these theories are based and with key influences on gender development, such as personality and the media.

3 **Self development**: the process of self development begins with *self-recognition* and *self-awareness*, leading to the emergence of various *self-concepts* (e.g. *self-esteem, self-efficacy, categorical self, psychological self, ideal self*). The self-concept is learned through the reactions of others (**Cooley**), comparisons with and expectations of others, and roles (**Kuhn**). Theoretical accounts of self development have come from **Erikson**, **Marcia**, **Rogers** and **Mead**. You should consider theories of adolescence (see below) because this is a key period in self development.

Adolescence, adulthood and old age

1 **Adolescence**: you should be familiar with theories and research related to personality change and social development in adolescence, for example, **Freud**, **Erikson**, **Marcia** and **Coleman**. Changes can be related to physical factors (e.g. puberty, self-image, gender differences), psychological factors (self-identity, cognitive development) and social factors (employment, friendships). A key question is whether adolescence is necessarily a time of storm and stress. Some psychologists agree (e.g. **Erikson**, **Rutter**), whilst others disagree (e.g. **Mead**, **Coleman**).

2 **Adulthood**: you should know **Erikson's** *stage theory of adulthood*, and alternatives such as **Levinson's** formulation based on *seasons*, **Gould's** *transitions* and **Duvall's** *family life cycle*. These focus on the general course of development whereas other approaches look at common events (*critical life event theory*: marriage, parenting, divorce, unemployment, bereavement and death, with research by **Holmes and Rahe**) or use universal principles (e.g. *social learning theory*) or concentrate on an aspect of development (e.g. intelligence).

3 **Old age**: you should be familiar with research related to cognitive, physical and social changes in old age. Theoretical accounts of ageing include *disengagement theory* (**Cumming and Henry**), *activity theory* (**Havighurst**, **Blau**), *social exchange theory* (**Dowd**) and *continuity versus discontinuity*. You should also consider issues related to society's view of ageing, and evidence from studies such as **Neugarten**, **Livson** and **Sheehy**.

Additional points for other candidates
NEAB
- The **Perspectives in Psychology module** (compulsory) includes: Erikson.

- The **Contemporary Topics in Psychology module** (see Unit 9) includes: human ageing and retirement. **Plus**: dementia, Alzheimer's disease and the frail elderly.

- The **Child Development module** includes: sociability and attachment, and cognitive, moral, gender and self development. **Plus**: issues in child development (developmental sequence, growth, maturation, critical/sensitive periods, research methods and their limitations, types of theoretical explanations) and language acquisition (see Unit 5).

- The **Psychology in Education** module (see Unit 9) includes: testing intelligence, gender differences and their effects on teaching and learning, and practical applications in education.

If you need to revise this subject more thoroughly, see the relevant topics in the *Letts* A-level Psychology Study Guide.

REVISION SUMMARY

OCSEB

- The **Developmental Psychology section** (compulsory) includes: attachment. **Plus**: structuralist and behavioural theories of development and child development research methods.

- The **Culture and Identity section** (compulsory) includes: gender identity.

- The **Psychology and Education specialist choice** (see Unit 9) includes: testing intelligence and practical applications in education.

QUESTIONS

1   'Mother love in infancy and childhood is as important for mental health as are vitamins and proteins for physical health' (Bowlby, 1951). Discuss.   (24)

AEB

2   (a) Describe any **one** theory of cognitive development.   (12)

    (b) Analyse applications of this theory to education.   (12)

AEB (specimen)

3   Discuss psychodynamic **and** social learning theories of moral development.   (24)

AEB

4   Describe and critically evaluate any one theory of psychological development in adulthood.   (24)

AEB

This module relates to all other areas of the syllabus. You should draw on a range of examples from your other psychological studies to support your arguments.

Approaches to psychology

❶ **Major theoretical orientations**: you should be critically familiar with the assumptions and contributions of the main theoretical orientations, namely the *behaviourist*, *humanistic* (person-centred) and *psychodynamic* approaches. Other approaches include: *biological*, *ethological*, *cognitive* and *sociocultural*.

❷ **The nature of the person**: there are certain key debates and issues in psychology: reductionism, free will versus determinism, nature versus nurture, objectivity versus subjectivity and nomothetic versus idiographic techniques. You should be able to present arguments representing both sides of these debates.

❸ **Individual, social and cultural diversity**: you should be familiar with explanations of individual, social and cultural diversity.

Controversies in psychology

❶ **Applications**: you should be acquainted with areas of 'controversial' psychological research, including advertising, propaganda, warfare and psychometric testing (personality and intelligence).

❷ **Psychology as a science**: you should be aware of the arguments for and against psychology as a science.

❸ **Biases in theory and research**: the main biases concern culture (e.g. the concept of the *extended self*, **Nobles**) and gender (e.g. *alpha-* and *beta-bias*, **Hare-Mustin and Marecek**). Various *androcentric* theories could be considered, such as those of **Freud, Erikson** and **Kohlberg**, as well as *androcentric* research (e.g. the use of male subjects). In contrast you should be familiar with *alpha-biased* views (e.g. **Gilligan**), and general approaches which have a gender bias, for example, the medical approach to psychological disorders.

Ethical issues in psychology

❶ **Human participants**: you should be aware of the ethical issues involved in psychological investigations which use human participants, and of attempts made to resolve these issues. You should also be familiar with appropriate ethical guidelines.

❷ **Non-human animals**: similarly you should be aware of the ethical issues involved in psychological investigations which use non-human animals, including the constraints and arguments for and against their use. You should again be familiar with the relevant ethical guidelines.

❸ **Responsibilities of psychologists in society**: you should be aware of the ethical responsibilities of psychologists with regard to wider social issues, including the ethics of socially sensitive research and issues of social control, such as 'alternative' sexuality and race-related research (e.g. race and IQ). Other areas of concern might include: child abuse, trauma victims, unemployment, divorce and mental retardation. A further responsibility of any researcher is to be sensitive to social and cultural diversity.

REVISION
SUMMARY

Additional points for other candidates

NEAB

*   The **Perspectives in Psychology module** (compulsory) includes: nature of scientific enquiry, key debates. **Plus**: social/historical context (Darwin, Freud, Wundt, Skinner, Rogers, concepts from computer technology); the biological approach: genetic and physiological basis of behaviour (genetics, evolution, twin studies, CNS, brain localization, hormones); the behaviourist approach (conditioning and social learning), the cognitive approach (computer analogies), and the person-centred approach (psychoanalytic e.g. Freud and Erikson, humanist e.g. Rogers and Maslow).

*   The **Research Methods and Data Analysis module** (compulsory) includes: code of ethics (see Unit 8).

OCSEB

*   The **Culture and Identity section** (compulsory) includes: cultural diversity. **Plus**: the psychometric approach (evaluation and application of tests), issues of gender identity (see Unit 6), and the implications of ethnocentrism and multiculturalism.

If you need to revise this subject more thoroughly, see the relevant topics in the *Letts* A-level Psychology Study Guide.

QUESTIONS

1 Critically consider the freedom versus determinism debate as it applies to psychology. (24)

AEB

2 Outline and assess any two psychological theories in terms of their gender bias. (24)

AEB (specimen)

3 'There are those who cling to the belief that human beings have some unique essence setting them quite apart from the rest of evolution, so lending colour to the liberationist claim that research with animals is not only morally wrong, but also of no practical value for people.' (Gray, 1986)

With reference to the issues raised in the above quotation, critically consider the use of non-human animals in psychological research. (24)

AEB

Research methods in psychology 8

REVISION
SUMMARY

The nature of psychological enquiry

❶ **Experimental investigations**: you should know the uses, advantages and limitations of *experimental* investigations, including *laboratory* and *field* methods. You should be familiar with relevant ethical considerations.

❷ **Quasi- and non-experimental methods**: you should know the uses, advantages and limitations of experimental investigations, including *natural experiments*, investigations using *correlational analysis, naturalistic observation, case studies* and *interviews* (surveys). You should be familiar with relevant ethical considerations.

The design and implementation of experimental and non-experimental investigations

❶ **Investigative design**: you should be able to select an investigative design that is appropriate to a particular research situation. You should be familiar with the relative merits and applications of different kinds of experimental design: *independent groups, repeated measures, matched participants* and special methods such as *pilot studies*.

❷ **Aims and hypotheses**: you should be able to generate appropriate research aims and formulate appropriate hypotheses, including *null, experimental/alternative* and *one-tailed* or *two-tailed* hypotheses.

❸ **Participants and materials**: you should be critically familiar with the procedures for selecting participants (*sampling*) and selecting materials.

❹ **Measuring and categorizing behaviour**: you should be aware of the problems of measuring and categorizing behaviour, to include the process of operationalizing variables or factors under investigation. You should also be familiar with levels of measurement (*nominal, ordinal, interval* and *ratio* scales).

❺ **Control**: you should be critically familiar with the various methods of minimizing the effects of situational variables, including *standardization* (for tests and for instructions), *counterbalancing* and *randomization*. You should also consider the relationship between researchers and participants, including *demand characteristics* and *experimenter effects*.

❻ **Issues of research design**: you should be acquainted with key issues related to research, such as *generalizability, participant reactivity, reliability* and *experimental* and *ecological validity*.

Data analysis

❶ **Descriptive statistics**: you should be critically familiar with measures of central tendency (*mode, median* and *mean*), measures of dispersion (*variation ratio, range, standard deviation*) and the use and interpretation of graphical methods (*histograms, bar charts, frequency polygons* and *scattergraphs*).

❷ **Inferential statistics**: you should be able to use and interpret various two-sample statistical tests of difference (*Mann–Whitney U test, Wilcoxon matched pairs signed ranks test*, and *sign test*), a test of association (*chi-squared test*) and a test of correlation (*Spearman's rho*). You should know how to interpret the *statistical significance* of your results, and should understand issues related to the interpretation of significance, e.g. *Type I and II errors*, and *degrees of freedom*.

❸ **Other methods of qualitative and quantitative analysis of data**: you should be familiar with methods of interpreting interviews, case studies and observational studies (e.g. *content analysis*).

If you need to revise this subject more thoroughly, see the relevant topics in the *Letts* A-level Psychology Study Guide.

REVISION SUMMARY

Additional points for other candidates

NEAB

• The **Research Methods and Data Analysis module** (compulsory) includes: experimental and non-experimental methods of investigation (to include psychometric methods), the design and implementation of investigations and data analysis. **Plus**: parametric and non-parametric tests (related and independent *t*-tests, Pearson's product moment) and ethical issues (see Unit 7).

OCSEB

• The **Methodology section** (compulsory) includes: experimental and non-experimental methods of investigation, the design and implementation of investigations and data analysis.

QUESTIONS

1 (a) State **one** feature of an experiment which distinguishes it from other kinds
   of research.   (1)

   (b) Describe **two** ways that field and natural experiments differ.   (2)

   (c) Suggest **one** advantage and **one** limitation of using the interview method of research. (2)

   (d) Outline **two** important ethical considerations which should be taken into account
   when planning research involving interviews.   (2)

2 A researcher wishes to explore the influence of peers on cognitive development in children aged between 6 and 10 years. She intends to do this by using interviews with children, questioning them on their views on moral problems such as whether or not it is acceptable for a child to cheat in a classroom test. The researcher intends to use a team of four colleagues to interview children in a group with peers and on their own.

   (a) Describe an appropriate way in which the researcher might select the children to take
   part in the study.   (2)

   (b) Justify the use of either an independent groups, repeated measures or matched
   participants design.   (3)

   (c) Explain how you would maximise reliability in the study.   (3)

   AEB (specimen)

3 A psychologist wanted to determine whether a certain species of animal in captivity displayed more settled behaviour after the introduction of a new programme aimed to reduce their distress. To investigate this she organized a team of observers to watch the animals in their zoo pens both before and after the new programme was introduced. They used the time sampling method to produce frequency counts of settled and unsettled behaviour.

   (a) Write a suitable null hypothesis for this study.   (1)

   (b) What is meant by *time sampling*?   (2)

   (c) Describe an alternative method by which the animals' behaviour could have been
   observed.   (2)

   (d) Why was it desirable to use a team of observers?   (3)

4 A psychology student devised a study to investigate the extent to which the personality trait of extraversion might be inherited. To do this she first asked members of her psychology class to complete a personality questionnaire measuring extraversion. She then asked each member of her class to take copies of the test home and supervise their parents, brothers and sisters (where applicable) when they answered the test. All who were approached to take the test were given the option of refusing to participate.
   All the class members were provided with standardized instructions on how to administer the personality test. Each person tested scored between 0 and 24, where the higher the number the more extravert a person is believed to be.

The test scores, for different relationship pairings, were compared using a Spearman Rank Order Correlation test with a directional hypothesis. The relationship pairings, number of such pairings and correlation coefficients are given below in Table 1.

Table 1 Relationship pairings, numbers of each relationship pair and correlations for extraversion

Relationship pairings	Number of pairs	Correlation coefficient
Mother–daughter	10	0.62
Mother–son	8	0.38
Father–daughter	10	0.27
Father–son	8	0.88

(a) In the context of statistical testing, what is meant by a one-tailed test? (1)

(b) For the study described above provide an appropriate hypothesis. (2)

(c) What level of measurement describes the scores from the personality test? Justify your answer. (2)

(d) Explain why it would be appropriate to use the Spearman Rank Order Correlation test on the data in this study. Justify your answer. (3)

(e) The student decided to use a significance level of 5 per cent. Explain what is meant by 'significance level' and why the student might have chosen a 5 per cent level. (4)

(f) Outline an appropriate way (other than tables) of displaying the relationship between the personality test scores of mothers and their daughters. Assume that the individual scores on the personality questionnaire were available for all who took the test. (2)

In order to test for significance, the correlation coefficients were compared to critical values shown in an appropriate statistical table, part of which is presented below.

Table 2 Critical values and significance levels for the Spearman Rank Order Correlation Coefficient

	Level of significance for one-tailed test		
N	0.05	0.025	0.01
7	0.71	0.79	0.89
8	0.64	0.74	0.83
9	0.60	0.68	0.78
10	0.56	0.65	0.75
11	0.53	0.60	0.71

(g) With the reference to the critical values given in Table 2 above, give the significance level for **each** of the correlation coefficients shown in Table 1. Write the details in your answer book. (4)

(h) Offer an explanation for the findings you have given in an answer to part (g) above that is **not** based on the inheritance of personality. (3)

(i) The student decided to conduct a case study on one of the mother–daughter pairings used in the study described earlier.

   (1) Outline how you would go about conducting such a case study. (4)

   (2) Identify two weaknesses of the case study approach. (2)

   (3) Discuss what could be gained from the case study that could not be obtained from the correlational study described above. (3)

NEAB

Letts
Q&A

9 *Applied and contemporary psychology*

REVISION SUMMARY

Contemporary topics in psychology   *(NEAB module PS03)*

❶ **Human relationships** (described in Unit 1).

❷ **Human ageing** (described in Unit 6).

❸ **Psychology and work** (described in Psychology and organizations, below).

❹ **Substance abuse** (described in Psychology and health, below).

❺ **Psychology and paranormal phenomena**: you should be familiar with the evidence for and against *extrasensory perception (ESP), telepathy, clairvoyance, precognition, psychokinesis (PK)* and *psi-phenomenon*. You should consider the relationship between ESP and personality, and the question of training for ESP. You should be aware of the research methods used in parapsychology (*case studies, field investigations, experimental procedures*), methods used in specifically in ESP research (*free-response tests, restricted choice experiments, matching tests*), methods used in PK research (*micro-methods* – standard dice test, *macro-methods* – movement of objects), and research problems (e.g. *experimenter effects, demand characteristics*).

Psychology and organizations   *(NEAB module PSO3, OCSEB specialist choice)*

❶ **Motivation and job satisfaction**: you should be familiar with *need theories* of motivation (e.g. **Maslow, Alderfer, McClelland**), *job design theories, cognitive theories, reinforcement theories* and research on the relationship between motivation and job performance. You should also be aware of theories of *job satisfaction* (e.g. **Herzberg**, *need-satisfaction, social information processing*), including ways to assess and increase job satisfaction, *organizational commitment* and employee attendance.

❷ **Personnel selection**: methods include the use of written materials, interviews, situational exercises and letters of reference. You should be familiar with equal opportunity issues, how jobs are defined (e.g. *job analysis*) with specific psychometric tests of aptitude and personality.

❸ **Group processes**: you should be aware of theory and research related to inter- and intragroup behaviour, roles, norms, group cohesiveness, team work and leadership (see Unit 1).

❹ **Organizational issues (OCSEB only)**: you should be familiar with theory and research related to *communication in organizations*, and the goals and evaluation of *organizational change, dynamics, culture* and *health* (including ergonomics, the work environment, health and safety at work and occupational diseases).

❺ **Decision making (OCSEB only)**: you should be critically aware of research relevant to decision making (see Unit 5).

Psychology and health   *(NEAB module PS08 and PS03, OCSEB specialist choice)*

❶ **Pain (NEAB PS08 and OCSEB)**: you should be familiar with theories and research related to pain: how people interpret symptoms, understand explanations and manage pain (*behavioural* and *biomedical* models, *gate control theory, specificity* and *pattern theories*).

❷ **Psychological aspects of illness (NEAB PS08 and OCSEB)**: you should be aware of how psychological factors affect patient/practitioner relationships, *health promotion* (*Yale model* – **Hovland**, *health belief model* – **Rosenstock**), *compliance* with medical requests, psychological effects of hospitalization, and *sick role behaviour*. You should understand the effects of psychological factors on physical conditions (e.g. diabetes and asthma) and chronic ill-health problems (e.g. coronary heart disease (CHD), cancer and AIDS), and the problems of coping with such illnesses.

❸ Lifestyles and health (NEAB PS08 and OCSEB): you should be aware of how lifestyle (e.g. exercise, nutrition, body weight, culture, risk-taking) affects health. You should be familiar with theories of CHD, cancer, eating disorders and lifestyle change (*self-efficacy theory* – **Bandura**, *reasoned action theory* – **Ajzen and Fishbein**, *health belief model* – **Becker**, and *preventative health action model* – **Tones**).

❹ Stress and illness (NEAB PS08 and OCSEB): you should be familiar with the nature and sources of stress, its health consequences, and methods of coping with and managing stress (see Unit 3).

❺ Substance use and abuse (NEAB PS03 and OCSEB): you should consider solvents, tobacco, nicotine, alcohol, stimulants and hallucinatory and hard drugs. You should understand the concepts of addiction, physical and psychological dependence, tolerance and withdrawal, why people use drugs and individual susceptibilities (e.g. heredity factors, personality characteristics, social influences/norms). You should be aware of treatment techniques (*aversion strategies, self-management strategies*) and prevention techniques (*fear-arousing appeals, health promotion, social 'inoculation'*).

❻ Health and illness (NEAB PS08 only): you should critically understand historical and current perspectives of health psychology: the *biomedical* model (with roots in Cartesian dualism), the *biosocial* model and *humanistic* and alternative approaches (e.g. aromatherapy, colour therapy, visualization, meditation, yoga). You should consider the new public health movement, and influences on epidemiology and social policy.

❼ Organizational health (OCSEB only): You should be aware of research around the issue of organizational health, such as *sick building syndrome* and problems of *population density* (see **Organizational issues** in 'Psychology and organizations' above).

Psychology and education   (*NEAB module PS09, OCSEB specialist choice*)

❶ Assessing learning: you should be familiar with assessment methods (*diagnostic, formative, summative, criterion* and *norm referenced*), the measurement of intelligence and other skills and abilities (using tests, interviews, observation, parental discussion) and of the relationship between ability and school performance.

❷ Promoting effective learning: you should be acquainted with investigations of how pupils learn, including psychological learning theories and teaching strategies such as: matching learning to the learner, *cognitive conflict*, co-operative learning, shared linguistic meanings, *complex learning*, *discovery learning* and the need for feedback.

❸ Teaching and learning interactions: you should be aware of the effects on school performance of cultural and developmental factors, teaching and learning styles, individual differences, teacher expectations, the pupil's self-concept, labelling, gender differences, prejudice and (**OCSEB only**) design.

❹ Motivational factors in learning: you should consider the use of rewards, praise, sanctions, encouragement, discipline, rules, empowerment and the relationship between stress and performance.

❺ Behaviour problems: you should be aware of methods of measuring classroom behaviour (e.g. observation, schedules, naturalistic settings, sociograms, self-report questionnaires) and the various difficulties (e.g. reliability of observers). You should consider methods of modifying behaviour, including the role of the educational psychologist (e.g. with truants and disciplinary problems), role expectations between teachers and pupils, and the teacher's use of non-verbal communication.

REVISION SUMMARY

If you need to revise this subject more thoroughly, see the relevant topics in the *Letts* A-level Psychology Study Guide.

6 **Reading (NEAB only)**: you should be familiar with psychological approaches to the teaching of reading, including diagnostic assessment, skills analysis, goal setting, graded targets, structured reading programmes, real books, phonics and whole word teaching methods. You should consider the subskills of reading (visual, auditory and cognitive aspects) and their implications for an understanding of dyslexia.

7 **Special Educational Needs (NEAB only)**: see Unit 4, learning difficulties.

Psychology and the environment   (*OCSEB specialist choice*)

1 **Effects on behaviour**: you should be familiar with psychological studies of climate (weather), noise, urban living, crowding, personal space, territoriality, architecture and design, and the effects these have on cognition, perception, attitudes and environmental stress. You should be aware of the applications of this research.

2 **Consumer behaviour**: you should know research on and applications of models of consumer behaviour, market segmentation, market research and buyer's behaviour.

Psychology and sport   (*OCSEB specialist choice*)

1 **Motivation**: (described in Unit 2).

2 **Social processes**: you should be familiar with audience effects (the effect of the audience on the performer and the performer on the audience), leadership (see Unit 1), group processes (see Unit 2), theories of aggression (see Unit 1) and the effect of attributions (see Unit 1).

3 **Learning**: (conditioning, described in Unit 2) and cognitive style (e.g. effect of expectations).

QUESTIONS

1 (a) Outline the features of any **two** parapsychological phenomena. (4)

   (b) In writing to a person who did not believe in the existence of paranormal phenomena, what might a parapsychologist put in a letter defending her belief in paranormal phenomena? Refer to empirical evidence in your letter. (8)

   (c) Write a letter of reply from the point of view of a psychologist, denying the existence of paranormal phenomena. Refer to empirical evidence in your answer. (8)
   NEAB

2 (a) Explain what is meant by *absenteeism* in a work-related context and give **two** explanations for its occurrence. (4)

   (b) On leaving the factory where he worked, an employee remarked: '... the only reason I go to work is for the pay, it's as simple as that'.

   (i) Making reference to theories of motivation, discuss **two** reasons, other than financial payment, that may encourage people to work. (6)

   (ii) Discuss how research and theory in psychology may be used to increase an individual's job satisfaction at work. Make reference to empirical studies in your answer. (10)
   NEAB

3 *'OUCH!*
The most pervasive symptom in medical practice, the most frequently stated 'cause' of
disability and the single most compelling force underlying an individual's choice to seek or
avoid medical care is ... PAIN.' (Karoly, 1985)

  (a) Describe a number of studies or approaches to the management and control of pain. (8)

  (b) Evaluate these studies or approaches. (10)

(HINT: You may wish to consider their effectiveness, the methodology used to test the
approaches, the perspectives on which the approaches are based and ethical issues.)

  (c) Identify one cause of acute (not chronic) pain and suggest a cognitive coping strategy
     that can be applied specifically to this type of problem. (6)

                                                                     OCSEB

4 (a) Name and describe **two** different teaching styles. (6)

  (b) Evaluate how each of the teaching styles you have described in your answer to
     part (a) might affect students' motivation. Refer to theory and empirical evidence
     in your answer. (14)

                                                                      NEAB

5 *Animals go on rampage in department store*

Dear Sir/Madam,

I work as an Assistant Manager at a local department store. Yesterday there was a small fire
in the store, and although the fire itself caused no injuries, when people tried to get out, a
number of them were trampled in the rush and they were taken to hospital. The local
newspaper printed the story with the above headline. The store manager has instructed me to
take responsibility to ensure this never happens again, but I'm unsure where to start. I need
the help of a psychologist to tell me how people behave in crowds in emergency situations,
so I can work on an appropriate strategy.

Yours faithfully,

John H. (Assistant Manager)

  (a) Review a number of psychological studies that are relevant to the behaviour of crowds
     in emergency situations. (8)

  (b) Evaluate these studies (where appropriate) in relation to

     (i) their conclusions;

     (ii) their methodologies;

     (iii) ethical issues;

     (iv) psychological perspectives. (10)

  (c) Based on the evidence you have presented, suggest an 'evacuation message' that the
     assistant manager could read out over the public address system. (6)

                                                                OCSEB

Answers

1 SOCIAL PSYCHOLOGY

Question 1

Examiner's tip Part questions are presented to help you focus on the different elements of a question and therefore achieve higher marks. This particular question could be 'Discuss what psychologists have found out about the reduction of prejudice and discrimination'. With essay questions many candidates overlook key issues and lose marks. Therefore you are directed in part (a) to describe the key terms. Parts (b) and (c) both require description and evaluation (Skills A and B).

Part (b) asks for one study only; other studies may be used as a means of evaluation but credit will only be given if this is made explicit. You should also note that this question is concerned solely with the reduction of prejudice and discrimination, therefore any theory or research related to the causes of prejudice will gain no credit unless it is made specifically relevant to the question.

Part (c) refers to 'attempts' therefore you should present more than one reason and your arguments should be psychologically-informed rather than anecdotal. In this part of the question it may be relevant to discuss causes of prejudice in the sense that the resilience of such causes may be one reason why attempts to reduce prejudice fail.

(a) Prejudice is an attitude held, prior to direct experience, towards a group or individual simply on the basis of group membership. Discrimination is the behaviour arising from a prejudice. It leads to the unequal treatment of individuals or groups on the basis of arbitrary characteristics.

Examiner's tip For each definition there is a maximum of 2 marks available. This maximum is awarded for a 'psychologically informed definition'. Where a definition is good but lacks psychology it will receive only 1 mark, for example, 'prejudice means prejudging someone'.

(b) Sherif et al. (1961) organized a field experiment called the 'Robber's Cave Experiment'. They invited a group of twenty-two 11-year-old boys to a summer camp and organized their accommodation so that there were two groups. Activities for the two groups were organized in such a way as to create a strong sense of intergroup rivalry and prejudice. The final stage of the experiment involved reducing both this prejudice and the resulting discrimination.

Examiner's tip This is an obvious study for students to choose because most textbooks provide lengthy descriptions and evaluations of it. However, a large part of the study involved creating the prejudice in the first place and therefore some candidates will be tempted to waste time describing this part of the study which is not relevant to this question. It would be hard to award full marks to such an answer because it would lack selectivity.

Sherif *et al.* first of all tried to see if contact alone would reduce the conflict they had created. For example, they organized various group activities for the boys such as filling out questionnaires, watching movies, having a fourth of July party and taking meals together. However, such occasions only served as opportunities to continue their fighting.

The second method was to introduce superordinate goals. These are goals which can only be achieved through joint co-operation. For example, the tank for their drinking water sprung a leak and all the children assisted in the repair. Also, on the way to a special overnight camp one of the buses broke down and they all had to help push.

At the end of the camp Sherif *et al.* assessed the friendships and found that the children still preferred members of their ingroup but they also expressed liking for members of the outgroup, demonstrating that their prejudices had been reduced. They also no longer expressed hostile attitudes towards the outgroup. In the bus going home some boys sat next to members of the other group; this shows that <u>discrimination</u> was also reduced.

This study has been criticized in terms of ethics because it involved manipulating children's attitudes in a negative way. It is impossible to assess whether there were any long-lasting effects on the participants. The experimenters gained parental consent though they did not fully inform parents about the aims of the study.

The results have value because of the real life setting. Other studies, such as Aronson *et al.*'s 'Jigsaw method', confirm that superordinate cooperative activities help decrease prejudice.

Examiner's tip The answer is coherent and well organized, and it communicates a critical understanding and the ability to be selective. The last two paragraphs are critical in providing some evaluation, both negative and positive, of the research. This lifts a rather average answer into the top band.

If you did write about more than one study, the examiner would only credit the best one covered. This is not a good exam strategy as you waste time writing material which will receive no marks. It is better to use the time thinking or writing notes to decide which study you know best in terms of both description and evaluation.

Alternatively, include the other studies but make sure you explicitly use them to evaluate the first, as has been done here with Aronson *et al.*'s research. In this case all material will be creditworthy.

(c) There are six arguments which should be considered.

Examiner's tip This is a very useful way to begin because it helps organize the subsequent material and indicates to the examiner that you have thought about what follows.

First, the processes involved in prejudice formation are inevitable and therefore resist reduction. They arise from the way that people think about the world and generate expectations from schema and stereotypes. Stereotypes and social identity produce biases towards groups of people. When this is coupled with hostility, intergroup conflict results.

Examiner's tip This is a cause of prejudice but has been used relevantly here. The same is true for the next point.

Second, people are reluctant to change their attitudes because they are like a pack of cards: if you pull one out a whole lot of others may fall down. For example, if you decide not to feel prejudiced about women this may lead to conflicts with your father who thinks that a woman's place is in the home.

Third, prejudices have positive as well as negative effects and therefore people resist reducing them. One way that prejudices are positive is that they increase a person's sense of self-esteem by creating a sense of ingroup favouritism or pride. Prejudices also simplify perceptions of the world making life more manageable. They can provide a useful outlet for aggression.

Fourth, attempts to reduce prejudice through cooperative activity may only have limited effects. Participants learn to decrease the prejudice they feel towards particular individuals but not towards the whole group. Stouffer *et al.* (1949) found

35

that racial prejudice amongst soldiers diminished in battle but this did not extend to relations back at base.

Fifth, increased contact may result in increased conflict. First-hand knowledge may increase aggression through resentment. For the minority group, integration may lead to lowered self-esteem because it emphasizes their inferior position, thus creating stronger hostilities. For example, Aronson et al. (1978) found that when non-white students worked with more advanced white pupils it only confirmed the ingroup and outgroup stereotypes held by both groups. To be successful, contact should be under conditions of roughly equal status and in a friendly rather than competitive context.

Finally, we should consider the fact that attempts to reduce prejudice do not always fail. Attitudes towards minority groups such as blacks, women or the disabled have improved but it is a slow process.

> **Examiner's tip** This answer contains clear examples of a top band answer. In terms of Skill A, it demonstrates a good understanding of relevant material. Skill B is demonstrated through the coherence and construction of the answer as well as the use of empirical support and contrasting views. What the answer lacks in depth it makes up for in breadth. An alternative approach would be to discuss fewer attempts but provide more detail for each, including further empirical evaluation (negative and positive).
>
> In part (c) if only one attempt at reduction is discussed then you would not get marks in the top range because the question asks for attempt<u>s</u>.

Question 2

> **Examiner's tip** This is a popular area of the syllabus but often one which candidates answer using anecdotal evidence. Some 'common-sense' material may be useful but you must strive to include 'psychologically informed' arguments and empirical support.
>
> One key feature of the question to note is that two theories only are required. Other theories can be used as a means of evaluation but this must be explicitly stated. This is a useful strategy because candidates are often very good at describing (Skill A) the selected theories but not evaluating them (Skill B).
>
> A theory may be any structured body of facts and not necessarily one that has a name and/or is associated with a psychologist. Therefore you might choose to describe interpersonal relationships in terms of proximity, similarity, complementarity, competence and so on.
>
> Another key feature of the question is that it refers to 'interpersonal relationships'. Interpersonal attraction is the formation stage alone whereas 'relationships' includes maintenance and dissolution as well. Any discussion of initial attraction alone would not gain much credit.

Outline answer

1 Define the key term 'interpersonal relationships':
  - Should explain the whole process: initial attraction, maintenance and dissolution.
  - The term 'relationships' can cover friendships, intimate relationships, love and marriage.

2 Theory 1: Equity Theory proposed by Walster *et al.* (1978).
  - Description: people strive for a balance in relationships, they maximize rewards and minimize unpleasant aspects of a relationship.
  - Positive evaluation: can explain initial attraction – the 'matching hypothesis'; can explain maintenance – e.g. trading off unpleasant domestic tasks; can

explain dissolution – equity must be continually bargained for or the relationship will fail.

- Research support: Murstein (1972) and Silverman (1971) found empirical evidence of similarity in terms of physical attraction between pairs. Silverman's study had ecological validity. Thibaut and Kelley's Social Exchange Theory is very similar and covers the whole of social interaction.

- Negative evaluation: Walster *et al.*'s (1966) computer dance participants sought the most attractive partners rather than those who were most similar. The idea that people are able to calculate costs and rewards might be very difficult in practice.

3   Theory 2: Byrne–Clore Reinforcement-Affect Model (1970).

- Description: we learn to associate certain feelings (affect) with people who reward (reinforce) us. Therefore we come to like someone with whom we associate positive feelings.

- Positive evaluation: similarity leads to positive attitudes (give examples). Can relate to equity theory. When reinforcement ceases the relationship may break down, though other factors such as interdependence may have developed and can explain why people stay together.

- Empirical support: Veitch and Griffiths (1976): good news and bad news. Rabbie and Horowitz (1960): liking increased when subjects did better on a game-like task. Nesselrode (1967) found that stable marriages were more likely between similar people. Has real-life validity.

- Negative evaluation: Bogus stranger methods, as used in some of above studies, lack realism (Duck, 1992). The concept of reinforcement is rather loosely defined.

4   General considerations:

- It is very difficult to study relationships.

- Difficult to make generalizations because there are wide individual and cultural differences.

Examiner's tip   The two theories selected are good because they are distinctly different. There could be some attempt to contrast them with each other. If the two theories were more similar (e.g. equity and social exchange) there could be some attempt to express their similarities and mention other theories as a means of assessing their value.

Question 3

Examiner's tip   The instruction to 'critically consider' implies that you should (1) demonstrate your knowledge and understanding of relevant research and (2) present its strengths and limitations. 'Research' can mean empirical and/or theoretical material. Therefore you could present empirical studies and evaluate their methodology or contribution to theories. Alternatively you could present theories and evaluate these in terms of studies which support or refute the theories.

If you use evidence related to conformity (the absence of independence) make sure you make it explicitly relevant or it will not receive credit.

The concept of independence can be defined as a resistance to social influences. Therefore we can look at social influences and how people resist them.

Answers to Unit 1

Early social-psychological experiments were concerned with the degree of obedience and conformity that people showed. One of the best known studies was conducted by Milgram (1963). He recruited subjects and told them that they would work in pairs: one would be the teacher and the other the learner; in fact the subject who took the role of 'learner' was a confederate. The learner was strapped into a chair and the teacher was told by the experimenter to administer escalating electric shocks every time a mistake was made. 65% of the teachers continued to the highest level of shocks, showing surprising levels of obedience to authority.

Another classic experiment demonstrated conformity to group opinion. Asch (1955) arranged for groups of 7–9 subjects to participate in a study supposedly of visual perception. Each member of the group had to say out loud which line of three was the same length as the one on the stimulus card. In fact all of the group members except one were confederates and on critical trials had been instructed to give the wrong answer. Asch found that 75% of the subjects conformed at least once. The average rate was 37%.

Asch tried several variations and found that if even one other group member dissented this cut conformity rates considerably. Also, if group members were not face-to-face, conformity was reduced. This tells us something about independent behaviour. People are encouraged to be independent when others are also dissenting, though in a way this is just a different sort of conformity because the group now has two norms and the subject can choose which norm to conform to.

One important feature of conformity experiments is the idea that people conform in *ambiguous* situations – when they do not know how to behave they look to others for informational social influence. For example, Jenness (1932) asked students to estimate the number of beans in a bottle and then to discuss this with members of a group. When asked again to make an estimate, their guesses shifted towards the group mean.

One criticism of Asch's study, by Perrin and Spencer (1980), was that the effect was a 'child of its time'. Another criticism is that both Milgram's and Asch's studies may be experimental artefacts; people may not really behave like this but when put in an experiment they strive to help the experimenter and therefore seek cues about how to behave (demand characteristics). The studies may not represent human behaviour in real life but only in artificial, experimental situations. On the other hand, both studies may indicate some important aspects of human behaviour.

Both Milgram's and Asch's studies demonstrated independent behaviour as well as conformity/obedience because not all subjects conformed or were obedient. In fact in Asch's study there was more non-conformity than conformity. This suggests that we might benefit by looking at why some people in some situations are independent. We have already seen that conformity is high when everyone else is behaving the same or when a situation is ambiguous. We have also seen that people model their own independent behaviour on others – in Asch's experiment, people became less conformist when others where also acting independently. Gamson et al. (1982) demonstrated this behaviour. In their study, groups of nine subjects were asked by a (fictitious) public relations firm, MHRC, to discuss a legal case involving a Mr C. It

became apparent that MHRC was trying to manipulate the subjects into producing a video tape expressing negative attitudes about the defendant in the case. This led some group members to object or 'rebel'. At the end of the experiment the group was asked to sign an affidavit giving MHRC permission to use the video tape in a trial. In cases where sufficient numbers of the group had rebelled, the whole group conformed to this lack of obedience to authority, but some groups did sign presumably because the majority in those groups did not have anti-authoritarian values.

Latané's (1981) law of social impact proposes that the amount of influence that others exert depends on three factors: the strength, the number and the immediacy of those exerting social pressure. This principle was derived mainly from studies of bystander intervention where it has been noted that people are unlikely to intervene in an emergency when everyone else is doing nothing (pluralistic ignorance), when no one is actually responsible (diffusion of responsibility) and the situation is ambiguous. One way to summon help from bystanders (i.e. elicit independent behaviour) is to make a direct plea.

Another theory, the social influence model (SIM, Tanford and Penrod) describes the amount of influence in terms of group size and number of target persons. According to this model, as each person is added to the group social influence initially rises rapidly but then tails off, as new group members have less and less overall effect.

Research shows that some people are more helpful than others and the same can be said for independent behaviour. Some people are more non-conformist. For example, Burger and Cooper (1979) used a questionnaire to assess a subject's desire for personal control. They then showed the subjects a set of cartoons and asked them to rate these in terms of funniness. This was done with a confederate who was expressing his own (predetermined) opinions. Subjects who were high in their desire for personal control were less influenced by the confederate.

Cultural differences can also account for varying rates of independence. Milgram (1961) repeated his research with French and Norwegian subjects and found differences.

An important application of this research into independent behaviour is understanding how people can be helped to resist. One suggestion is that simply knowing the results of social psychology experiments warns people about human behaviour and helps them to resist. Subjects in Milgram's study said this afterwards. Another suggestion is that the presence of one dissenter can reduce obedience. Finally, research such as Milgram's has shown us that people obey leaders who are regarded as high in status. One way to reduce obedience is to reduce the apparent expertise of a leader or challenge their motives. Followers are then less likely to be obedient. It can be seen from this that Milgram's research was of some value.

We should distinguish between kinds of non-conformity; in some cases what appears to be non-conformity is in fact just conformity to a different set of norms. True independence means that you are following your conscience when determining how to behave. There are some people who deliberately select not to do things which are expected of them and this is often undesirable behaviour. There are also many important thinkers in history who have refuted thinking of their time, for example, Galileo and Darwin. The problem lies in knowing when to conform and when not to.

| **Examiner's tip** | This is tending towards the anecdotal but is well argued and relevant. Be careful when including material which lacks psychology. |

In conclusion, the question of independent behaviour is very involved. It can be argued that it is more useful and positive to concentrate on the reasons why people exhibit independent behaviour rather than to demonstrate how obedient or conformist they are.

Letts
Q&A

What this essay lacks in coherence it makes up for in breadth. A considerable amount of credit goes to the persistent attempts to make material on conformity, obedience and bystander behaviour relevant to the question set. The studies used have been described in just enough detail to demonstrate knowledge and understanding (Skill A). It is sometimes tempting to write everything you know but this often reveals a lack of selectivity.

There is a good amount of critical comment, for example, the use of theory (Latané), some criticism of methodology (demand characteristics), mention of factors which moderate conformity (personality differences, culture) and possible applications of such research. Note that applications can be Skill A (accurate description/knowledge), but they are Skill B when used in an evaluative sense (as here), such as demonstrating the usefulness of some research or theory.

Question 4

This question can legitimately be answered by considering different explanations of aggressive behaviour as long as the discussion is placed in the appropriate media context. The more obvious approach will be to look at the argument that TV violence leads to aggressive behaviour, explaining relevant theories, describing empirical research and offering evaluations of both (= a critical discussion, Skill B).

One of the most important questions of our times is the extent to which violence on television increases levels of aggression in people, particularly among children. This is partly because of increases in the amount of violence we see today. Psychologists explain human aggression in terms of biological influences, such as hormones or genes, or environmental ones, such as frustration and learning. One of the ways by which people might learn to be aggressive is through the media, especially television and videos.

Social learning theory explains how people learn in this way. They imitate behaviour they see in others because of vicarious reinforcement – if someone appears rewarded for violent behaviour (for example, increased status or success) this makes it more likely that an observer will imitate it.

Bandura et al. (1963) did an experiment to demonstrate this. They placed children in a room where an adult hit and shouted at a life-size doll. Later they observed the children at play and saw that these children behaved more aggressively than a control group and also imitated specific acts of aggression. In further experiments, Bandura exposed children to filmed or cartoon models and found that the children were influenced by these though not as strongly as a live model. He also found that the status of the model was important, and that certain personality characteristics, such as low self-esteem, made observers more likely to imitate what they saw. Finally, a model who was punished was less likely to be imitated.

This study has been criticized most strongly for its lack of ethical consideration for the welfare of the children. It has also been suggested that the toys the children were given, such as a hammer, were strong cues for aggressive behaviour.

Note the evaluative comments; it is useful to get into the habit of making these, where possible, for every study mentioned.

Further evidence for direct imitation comes from case studies of copycat crimes. For example, in the James Bulger murder trial it was suggested that the horrific behaviour perpetrated by the boys was identical to things they had seen in a horror

video called 'Child's Play'. But not everyone who watches such videos goes out and behaves violently.

A lot of research has shown a correlation between television violence and aggressive behaviour; people who watch violent programmes are more likely to behave aggressively. This link may be because aggressive people prefer to watch violent programmes and therefore it is not watching TV which is causing aggression but vice versa. A related possibility is that violent programmes act as a trigger for people who have aggressive tendencies. An experimental study by Friedrich and Stein (1973) gives support to this view. They observed children in a nursery school for three weeks to establish how aggressive they were. After this the children were shown films which were either aggressive, prosocial, or neutral. In the last stage of the experiment the children were observed again. They found that the children who initially were above average in aggression were most affected by the violent cartoons, whereas those who were neutral did not react to either type of programme. This study is more realistic than Bandura's because it was conducted in the field.

The reason why some people are aggressive may be because they are born with an aggressive personality or they may have learned to be aggressive because that was the way their family behaved. When someone with an aggressive nature watches a violent programme this may increase the likelihood that they will commit a violent act or the programme may suggest particular actions to them. On the other hand, some people think that violent programmes might serve a useful cathartic purpose for people with aggressive natures.

There are reasons to suppose that watching violence affects all viewers, but that it affects less aggressive people less. First, the culture of the media establishes certain norms of behaviour, convincing us that such responses are acceptable. This may <u>disinhibit</u> our normal responses and increase our likelihood of responding aggressively. In America, the lawyer for a 15-year-old who shot his neighbour in the course of a burglary, claimed that the boy's sense of reality had been distorted through excessive exposure to television. Gerbner and Gross (1976) found that people who watch a lot of television rate the outside world as being more dangerous and threatening than it actually is. This has been called deviance amplification.

Second, violence on television may <u>desensitize</u> children by making them less emotionally upset by such acts and more able to tolerate them in real life. Drabman and Thomas (1975) demonstrated this in a number of experiments with primary school children. In each experiment the children were divided into groups and shown a film, which was either violent, or non-violent but exciting. The participants were then led to believe that they were responsible for monitoring the behaviour of two younger children viewed on a video and to summon help if any violence occurred. The younger children at first played quietly but became progressively more destructive, finally hitting each other and the TV camera. The researchers found that the children who had been exposed to the violent film were slower to respond, suggesting that the aggression they had viewed in the film made them more able to tolerate aggression in real life.

Third, watching violence may be <u>arousing</u>, which could increase the likelihood of aggressive behaviour. This will depend on what the child has learned about dealing with arousal and frustration through role models, especially their parents. It will also depend on the presence of environmental 'triggers'. Geen and Berkowitz (1967) demonstrated that frustrated participants will behave more aggressively. In their experiment those participants who watched a violent rather than an exciting film behaved more aggressively, and these participants behaved most aggressively towards a person with the same name (Kirk) as someone in the film they watched.

41

One of the problems with this research is that most of it is short term, which does not tell us how people are affected in the long run. Longitudinal studies such as by Eron *et al.* have found that children who watched violent programmes when aged 9 were more violent 10 years later than children who watched less.

It is important to distinguish between violent programmes as a primary cause of aggressive behaviour and as a contributory cause. They are probably not a primary cause but may increase levels of aggression particularly in susceptible people. One important factor may be the amount of punishment or reward that violent acts are seen to receive. Newson (1994) claims that when a victim is portrayed in sub-human ways we do not develop any empathy for them and therefore feel that no one really gets hurt. One of the differences between current video material and traditional gruesome fairy tales is that the viewer is more able to identify with the aggressor rather than the victim. Therefore a child is more likely to imitate a figure seen on television and is less likely to empathize with the victim.

The amount of exposure may also be critical because it limits the child's experience of the real world which would act as a counterbalance to fictional norms. Some exposure might actually be helpful, as in situations where children are shown how to deal with violence and how to respond to aggression from others or from within themselves. The media can also be used to show prosocial models which can balance the effects of violence.

In conclusion the question of whether the media might contribute to the development of aggressive behaviour is very complex although there is a lot of evidence to suggest that it does.

2 COMPARATIVE PSYCHOLOGY

Question 1

Two of the most important evolutionary pressures on any species are finding food and avoiding predation, because mistakes may prove fatal either through starvation or through getting killed. Therefore natural selection will favour successful predation and successful avoidance. Predator–prey relationships should be understood from the point of view of the predator and of the prey.

There are obvious behavioural characteristics necessary for successful predation, such as silent movement, stealth and a keen ability to detect movement and/or colour. These can be seen in birds of prey and members of the cat family. It is important for a predator to maximize the success of any attack because each attack uses up considerable energy in stalking and chasing. An individual who can locate prey successfully and mount the best surprise attack will be favoured by natural selection. Lions leave hunting to females possibly because the large mane of a male lion would disturb the prey. Lionesses cooperate in their hunt which enables them to tackle large prey such as water buffalo.

There are many fixed action patterns related to predation, such as the way a cat responds to a dangling piece of string by crouching down. It is obviously valuable for offspring to be born with successful predation techniques and natural selection would favour this. Predatory-like play seen in kittens may function to tune up these behaviours.

Examiner's tip The candidate has used anecdotal knowledge usefully, including appropriate psychological concepts.

Mimicry is a useful means of disguise for both predator and prey. For example, the cleaner wrasse attaches itself to bigger fish and performs a useful function of cleaning off parasites. The sabre-toothed blenny mimics the markings of the cleaner wrasse and therefore can approach the trusting bigger fish and take a bite before escaping. The angler fish dangles a worm-like bait on the end of a rod-like appendage. When a prey which itself normally feeds on worms approaches the bait, the angler fish eats it.

Examiner's tip In this area of the syllabus detailed and accurate examples take the place to some extent of named studies as they are a form of empirical evidence.

A useful strategy for prey is to mimic the markings of some other poisonous or distasteful animal, for example, one kind of harmless coral snake has the same colouring as its poisonous relative. This is called Batesian mimicry. In the case of those animals which are poisonous, they evolve bright colouring or warning displays as a means of advertising their danger and avoiding predation, because even if they did poison their predator it might be too late for the individual. Other animals can mimic such displays as well as the markings, for example, the hawkmoth caterpillar inflates and wags its head around like a snake and may even pretend to attack.

These strategies are clearly successful but it has to be asked how they started out as workable propositions. For example, a butterfly does not suddenly evolve a coloration which enables it to mimic a brightly coloured but poisonous relative. This change in coloration will have taken many years to evolve. During this time, their colour would have conferred no advantage since they did not look like their poisonous relatives and their bright coloration would have been positively disadvantageous because they would be more likely to be eaten. Another problem is the question of how the predator knows that a certain butterfly is poisonous. If they eat one they will die. This suggests that predator–prey recognition must be innate or learned through observation. Some warning patterns or displays are examples of sign stimuli and fixed action patterns – innate species-specific characteristics – which trigger an innate response. The advantage for both predator and prey is that this should enable a consistent and rapid response. Mullerian mimicry is based on such universal indicators of poisonous prey.

There is some evidence of innate recognition. For example, Tinbergen and Lorenz demonstrated that turkeys exhibit a fear response when they see the silhouette of a hawk (short neck, long tail) moving overhead but not when they see the same silhouette passing in the other direction, when it looks like a goose (long neck, short tail). They suggested that this is an innate response but others propose that it could be learned and might due to the fact that an object which appears blunt end first is more surprising.

| Examiner's tip | You might feel tempted to leave this area of innate behaviour out because there is considerable disagreement among psychologists. However, including arguments for and against is good evidence of Skill B, even if the issue is not resolved. |

Camouflage is another means by which prey evolve a means of avoiding predation. Some animals such as the squid have incredible systems which enable them to change colour and shape to avoid detection.

Blanchard et al. (1990) listed four key behaviours shown by animals in response to predation. These are flight, freeze, defensive attack and setting predators against each other. The most common response is flight. This is obviously adaptive behaviour because it should enable the animal to get away. However it is not always successful because such behaviour elicits a response from the predator, i.e. to chase.

A freeze response may be an effective alternative. The animal, such as a mouse, sits still, becoming more tense as the predator approaches. This is in readiness for sudden escape which may surprise the predator. A variation on the freeze response is the gazelle's stott. This might appear to be a way of confusing an enemy but Caro (1986) observed that stotting appears to inform the predator (e.g. a cheetah) that it has been spotted and this usually results in the predator abandoning the hunt. The stott may be a way of communicating to the predator that it has been seen. The freeze response may also be an attempt by the prey to assess whether it has in fact been spotted by the predator.

A freeze posture may turn into defensive attack when the prey actually lunges suddenly towards the predator creating a defensive response from the predator and giving the prey a chance to flee. In some animals there is an intermediate state between freeze and attack where the animal indicates intention to act. For example, a cat hisses, its hairs stand up and the cat arches its back, turning sideways, all in attempt to appear larger. Some moths expose eye-like spots on their wings. These may startle a predatory bird giving the moth a chance to escape.

The final anti-predator technique can be seen in rabbits. They scream when attacked thus attracting other predators which then attack the original predator in competition for the prey, giving the prey a chance to escape.

Warning systems may have other effects, such as preventing attack in the first place. One or more members act as a look out. This is particularly necessary when animals are feeding, for example, when a flock of geese are grazing at least one member keeps watch and when that individual starts to feed another one takes over as look out.

In other social groups the flight response may confuse the predator and therefore be successful. Sherman studied squirrels and showed that one of them gives a high pitched call to warn of trouble and then the whole group dashes for cover. Such a scuffle confuses the predator and also protects the animal who gave the warning who might otherwise have been picked off. The schooling of fish has a similar effect.

Vervet monkeys have quite a sophisticated system of alarm calls. Seyfarth and Cheyney (1980) have observed three different types of call each related to a different predator: the eagle, leopard and python. This is important because the monkeys need to behave differently depending on which animal is near. If it is an eagle, they need to look up and run for cover; if it is a python they should look on the ground.

There are many other ways of avoiding predation that animals have evolved such as feeding at night, living in burrows and living alone (less easy to detect). In all of the strategies described it can be seen that any behaviour which results in successful attack or avoidance of predation will be favoured by natural selection because it increases the individual's chances of surviving to reproduce. In the case of group strategies, these can be explained in terms of kin selection (altruism at the level of the genes) or reciprocal altruism.

Examiner's tip Candidates answering questions from this area of the syllabus need to beware of offering material which is more common sense than psychological. You should use specific, well detailed examples and employ psychological terminology, as has been done here. This particular answer offers a good breadth of knowledge, discussing a large number of predator–prey behaviours within the context of evolutionary pressures. An alternative approach might have been to describe fewer behaviours but give more detailed examples of these and discuss relative advantages and disadvantages.

Question 2

Examiner's tip Part (a) calls for two short descriptions, as indicated by the total of 6 marks available. Part (b) involves both the description of one psychological explanation for differential investment (Skill A) and evaluation of this explanation (Skill B). Such evaluation could involve the use of other explanations by way of contrast and assessment. However, credit can only be given where this evaluative use is explicit.

You should note that the question is related to the care of offspring, not to reproductive strategies. If you do include such material it must be made relevant to parental care. You should also note that the question does not say 'non-human' and therefore you would be credited for any material based on human as well as non-human behaviour.

(a) In most species the female makes the greater investment in the rearing of the young, in terms of time and sharing personal resources. This is the case in lionesses who live in a harem consisting of other females and their young. The females do all the hunting and the males help themselves once the kill is over. One or two males are associated with the harem but they are not concerned with the rearing of the young at all. The females provide milk for the very youngest cubs and then continue to feed them until they can catch their own food which they learn from joining the other lionesses in a kill. The harem protects the cubs from predation.

In some species the male makes the greater investment in parental care. For example, the male stickleback chooses a suitable territory at the beginning of the season and builds a funnel-shaped nest. He then courts a female and leads her to his nest where he stimulates her to deposit her eggs. The male then covers the eggs with his sperm and repeats this with other females. The male remains with the eggs until they hatch, fanning the eggs to keep them oxygenated. When the eggs hatch, the young are capable of fending for themselves and need no further parental care.

Examiner's tip In this part of the question it would be acceptable to describe any two different kinds of parental investment. For full marks the descriptions should be well detailed and coherent, reporting all important behaviours and demonstrating the roles of both sexes. No explanation of the behaviour is required.

(b) One explanation for the differential investment of males and females in the rearing of the young is that it is related to the form of fertilization. If a species has external fertilization, like the stickleback, then the male tends to be the one left caring for the young, whereas if fertilization is internal it is usually the female who takes care of the offspring.

Several theories have been proposed to explain this. Ridley's (1978) paternity certainty hypothesis proposes that a male is more likely to care for young when fertilization is external because this increases the certainty that the offspring are his own. In the case of internal fertilization the male can desert, knowing (or thinking) that the offspring are his. Dawkins and Carlisle (order of gamete release hypothesis) have suggested that both sexes prefer not to be left 'holding the baby' because this decreases their own chances of survival and future reproductive success. If the species uses internal fertilization this allows the male to get away first; with external fertilization the female can leave first. Williams' (1975) association hypothesis suggests that the adult who is left in close proximity to the embryo tends to take care of the young. Where external fertilization takes place this is the male; with internal fertilization this is the female.

The problem with all these theories is that there are exceptions to the rule that external fertilization leads to paternal care or that internal fertilization leads to maternal care. For example, the female jacana lays a clutch of eggs for each male in her harem and then leaves them for the male to incubate and rear entirely on his own. Ridley says there are at least 20 species where internal fertilization takes place yet the male is the one who makes the greater investment in paternal care.

In the case of the jacana the male role may be related to the method of combination. There are three variations in the ways that males and females combine which influences who does the caring. In polygynous species one male has exclusive rights to several females (a harem), as in deer or lions. In such cases the females do the caring because the male has already protected his investment. In polyandrous species one female mates with many males and therefore the male is most likely to do the caring, as in the seahorse and the jacana. In monogamous species one male mates exclusively with one female either for one or more seasons; this is associated with biparental care. Monogamy is rare in most animals but common in birds. When pair-bonding is for many seasons this minimizes one aspect of parental investment because they do not have to devote time and energy to locating and selecting a new mate each season.

Another problem with mode of fertilization explanations is that they do not account for biparental care (associated with monogamy) or cases where there is shared or no parental care. One example of shared care can be seen in many social insect groups such as ants and in other animals such as the mongoose. In these societies only one or two individuals mate and the rest of the society, who are genetically related, invest their resources in caring for the reproductive members.

This cannot be explained in terms of mode of fertilization but can be understood in terms of kin selection since those individuals who do not reproduce are still promoting their genetic line (inclusive fitness).

Many fish lay and fertilize their eggs and that is the end of their parental care. They protect their investment in ways other than parental care. There is a trade off between maximizing survival of the young and minimizing risk to the reproducer. An individual can either produce many offspring and invest little or no time (an r strategy), in which case the survival of the genes is ensured through sheer numbers. Alternatively an individual may produce only a very limited number of offspring but remain with them to increase the offspring's chances of survival (a K strategy). These strategies vary between species; most fish use an r strategy whereas most birds use a K strategy. The strategies also vary between the sexes — males produce many sperm at relatively little cost physiologically, females produce considerably fewer eggs which in all animals are larger than the sperm and contain nutrient substances, therefore their investment is greater. For both males and females natural selection should favour any method which promotes the survival of their genes. In males this may be achieved if their sperm fertilize as many eggs as possible or a male may seek to fertilize fewer eggs but remain with the offspring through some of their development.

The cuckoo is another example of no parental care. The female cuckoo lays its eggs in the nest of another bird and leaves the care to the foster parents. In this case the parents genetic interest is protected by having evolved a good means of substitute parental care. Maynard Smith says that male and female strategies (M and F strategies) should form an evolutionarily stable combination. For example, if a female has produced some offspring, it would be a bad policy to abandon them in order to start breeding again because the chances of survival are better for those already born. However, if the female could depend on the male to care for the offspring, the best strategy for the female is to start producing some more offspring. For the male, the best strategy is to depend on the female so that he can go off to reproduce elsewhere. For this reason the mode of fertilization approach is likely to be right much of the time.

However, even where internal fertilization takes place the male may not be guaranteed paternity, which was suggested by Ridley's paternity certainty hypothesis. In which case even with internal fertilization the male should stay with the female for some time in order to ensure the offspring are his own. Parker (1978) showed that when two male dungflies mate with the same female, the sperm of the second male fertilize most of the eggs. This is called sperm competition. It can be counteracted by having copulation in private or remaining with the female after intercourse. For example, male houseflies remain in the copulation position for an hour after the sperm have been transferred. In some species a strategy called 'sneak copulation' has developed, where a second male manages to have intercourse covertly. Some male elephant seals pretend to be females and are then able to join a harem for sneak copulation when the bull is occupied elsewhere. In order to counteract this males must be very possessive of their females.

We have seen that there are a number of different explanations for the differential investment of males and females in parental care to maintain the optimum balance between (1) survival of offspring at the expense of the reproducer's own survival and (2) future reproductive success. It seems that mode of fertilization is a useful way of explaining the outcome but that other factors must be considered as well.

Examiner's tip This answer demonstrates a high degree of knowledge and is focused on parental care rather than the wider issue of reproductive strategies. The discussion is coherent, well-detailed, accurate and uses psychological concepts. Skill B is shown by the evaluation of the original explanation through the use of examples and alternative explanations. If these examples and alternative explanations had been included but not explicitly used to evaluate the mode of fertilization hypothesis, they would receive no credit.

Question 3

Examiner's tip The use of quotations in questions is a means of presenting a standard argument and asking the student to provide material in support of that viewpoint (Skill A) and in contrast to it (Skill B). For example, the quote from Ridley states that the laws of natural selection do not explain altruism, in which case how can it be explained? Your answer should show an understanding of the process of natural selection, how this might appear not to explain altruism, how altruism might be explained, and how theories derived from Darwin do in fact explain altruism. It is critical in questions which start out with a quotation that you make reference to the quotation. Therefore it is useful to break the quotation down and address each point.

In this question Skill A is demonstrated through knowledge and understanding of apparent altruism, and Skill B can be demonstrated by examining the way certain theories can or cannot account for apparent altruism.

A key point to note is that the question says 'non-human', therefore any reference to studies of human altruism would receive no credit.

Outline answer

1. Analyse the components of the quotation as suggested in the Examiner's tip.

2. Define altruism.
   - It is distinct from co-operation.
   - It involves a risk to the helper's survival/future reproductive success.
   - Give some examples.

3. Describe the process of natural selection.
   - Explain the process, e.g. a species evolves through survival of the fittest, or through strategies which promote inclusive fitness.
   - Define key terms, e.g. 'to evolve' and 'fittest' and 'inclusive fitness'.

4. Why might it be thought that natural selection <u>cannot</u> cause altruism?
   - Any behaviour which reduces an individual's capacity to reproduce should not be naturally selected.
   - Individuals are in competition to survive so why do they help each other?

5. How can altruism be explained in terms of natural selection?
   - Group selection theory (Wynne-Edwards) suggests that a species which behaves altruistically has better chances of survival. But this cannot be explained within natural selection theory because selection is at the level of the individual and not the group.
   - Reciprocal altruism (Trivers): altruists are likely to be helped in return so increasing their survival chances. However, this depends on recognition of individuals, which may occur through proximity and/or imprinting, smell (Greenberg, 1979) or the 'Green Beard Effect' (Dawkins, 1976).

- Inclusive fitness (Hamilton) and kin selection (Wilson): selection is about survival of genes not of individuals, therefore we can understand altruism when it is directed towards relatives. Altruistic <u>behaviour</u> only <u>appears</u> to be unselfish. This concept presupposes that individuals can recognize their relatives (see above). Sociobiological accounts assume that genes directly cause behaviour.

- Manipulated or induced altruism: explains cases of apparent <u>inter</u>species altruism in Darwinian terms, e.g. the cuckoo and its host, or parasites and their host. This fits the definition of altruism but is not in the genetic interest of the altruist.

6   Conclusion.

- It is referred to as 'apparent' altruism because the individual is actually acting selfishly in terms of its own gene pool.

- From the above, natural selection clearly can account for different kinds of apparent altruism.

- Sociobiological accounts are speculative, though they are supported by extensive observation.

Examiner's tip   An essay written following this outline would clearly relate to the question asked, breaking the statement down into its component parts and demonstrating a critical understanding of each. Skill B is demonstrated through the evaluation of each piece of evidence and in the appropriate selection of examples and theories.

Candidates who answer questions in this area of the syllabus are often either very competent or very weak. A typical weak response would consist of a definition of altruism (perhaps worth 2/3 marks) and a series of examples of apparent altruism (worth no more than 5 marks). Such an answer might be described as 'limited Skill A'.

Candidates who do not address the quote would be receive a maximum of 20 marks.

Question 4

Examiner's tip   Many candidates will be tempted to present their standard essay on teaching primates to speak but they may lose valuable marks in doing so. Which of course is why the examiner set this question – it enables differentiation between candidates because the better ones will adapt their knowledge to address the specific question whereas weaker ones will write more or less the same essay no matter what the question.

Part (a) starts with the word 'explain' which means that only Skill A is required.

Part (b) uses the phrase 'describe and evaluate' which warns you that this part of the question will be assessed in terms of Skills A and B. Therefore you should select a study which will provide sufficient scope for evaluation.

The use of the phrase 'comparative study of non-human animals' might be confusing as it suggests that you should use a study which compares two non-human animals whereas it is acceptable to use of a study of non-human behaviour which is being compared to human behaviour.

(a) Psychologists use the term 'communication' much as a lay person, to describe any activity where one individual or group passes information to another. This can be visual such as a frightened rabbit lifting its tail to show the white underpart; auditory such as birdsong as a means of finding a mate; olfactory such as a dog urinating to mark its territory; or kinaesthetic such as grooming as a means of confirming a dominance hierarchy.

Communication does not have to be intentional. For example, an animal who is excited may pant; this arises because of autonomic arousal and communicates to other individuals that the animal is excited. The communication is incidental to the autonomic activity.

Communication can be dishonest, for example, when one individual passes on information which will mislead the receiver. The markings on certain caterpillars mimic those of more dangerous animals to frighten off potential predators. Dishonest signalling may occur within a species as well, as when two male birds sing to compete for territories and mates, they may exaggerate reality. Dishonest signals are likely where competition exists either between or within species. Honest signals are related to co-operative behaviour.

Language is a set of arbitrary conventional symbols through which we convey meaning. It does not have to be spoken (vocal) but is always verbal (has a grammar). The term also has meaning for lay persons but psychologists have tried to be specific about what is and is not language. Hockett wrote a list of design features which should exist for a system of communication to be considered as a language. For example, the units must be arbitrary, they must have meaning rather than being referents, they must be learned and not inherited, meaning must be communicated by order (grammar), the system must be open-ended so that novel utterances can be produced, and it must allow prevarication (lying) and metalanguage.

Examiner's tip A good answer must reflect psychological rather than common-sense understanding. The use of illustrative examples is always a useful way to do this. A maximum of 6 marks is available for each definition, though two good definitions can only achieve the maximum of 10 marks.

The answer presented here treats the two terms in relative isolation. If you did make comparisons this would be a perfectly acceptable approach to explaining the terms but it is not necessary because comparison is a Skill B activity and only Skill A is examined here.

Hockett's list of design features is a good way of explaining what a language is; it does not need to be memorized and, as here, a few examples from it will suffice to demonstrate familiarity.

(b) The communication study I have chosen to describe and evaluate is Gardner and Gardner's (1969) research with Washoe. The first attempts to teach chimpanzees to speak involved trying to get them to say the words (Kellogg and Kellogg). The Gardners reasoned that chimpanzees may not have suitable apparatus for speaking but they do have nimble fingers, so it might be more successful to teach them sign language. They used American Sign Language (ASL or Ameslan). This language is largely iconic (the hand gestures look like what they represent) but some of it is arbitrary, which is a critical feature in distinguishing between using language and just communication.

This is a comparative study because the Gardners were investigating the claim that language is uniquely human. If Washoe could be trained to use language then language is not species-specific to humans.

Examiner's tip This is a good demonstration that the candidate has thought about the question and understands the concept of a comparative study.

Washoe, a female chimp, was taught from the age of one using operant techniques, such as tickling her as a reward. She was treated like a child and all conversation with her was in ASL. Her language development followed similar lines to a human child's acquisition. She learned and used words spontaneously and produced novel combinations of words such as 'open food drink' to mean open the fridge. By the age of four she had mastered over 100 signs.

Having described the study the candidate now goes on to evaluate it in terms of what the study has or has not demonstrated, and later to consider methodological problems.

The key question is whether Washoe's use of words constitutes language. It showed some elements of language such as displacement; she talked about things that were not there, but bees do the same in their dances. A key element that was missing from Washoe's communication was consistent order (grammar). For example, she would say 'go sweet' or 'sweet go'. Aitchison (1983) has suggested some reasons why Washoe did not develop grammatical language. It may be that the Gardners never consistently rewarded order, or it may be that sign language makes it difficult to be consistent because some deaf people also find this difficult. Alternatively it may be that she was simply incapable of acquiring grammar which means that it could be a uniquely human ability as Chomsky suggests – humans have innate brain structures which enable them to produce grammatical language. However, the Gardners claimed in later research that Washoe did use grammar.

There are a number of criticisms of this study. First of all, it was a case study and therefore we should be careful about making generalizations, though other studies of chimpanzees and other primates do support the view that they cannot develop grammatical language. Second, we must ask whether the animals in any of these studies 'cheated', like Clever Hans who picked up non-verbal signals from his trainer and therefore appeared to be able to add. Washoe was tested under double blind conditions where the Gardners could not see the objects she was being asked to name. She still could correctly answer more than half of the questions put to her.

Finally there is the question of ethics: is it reasonable to conduct such research? What happens to animals like Washoe? Researchers have a responsibility to care for and entertain these animals who have become used to a rich human environment. Washoe was featured in a BBC *Horizon* programme and shown living with other chimps in four rooms in a university psychology department. They are given playthings and dressing up clothes. At meal times they feed themselves and ask for more food.

The ultimate means of assessing the research is to ask whether the means can justify the ends. It still is not clear whether animals can use language but the answer is probably no. On the other hand such research may enable us to have a glimpse into another world. Therefore the importance of the work lies not just in what it tells us about language but in what it tells us about chimpanzees.

One of the strong points about this answer is the considerable amount of evaluative material which has been included. Many candidates will be able to describe such a study reasonably well but not to show a critical appreciation of it.

The last point about whether or not animals have language could have been spelled out further but the answer nevertheless fits the descriptor of a top band Skill A and B answer (accurate, well-detailed knowledge showing good understanding, few omissions, relevant theories/concepts/applications and coherent elaboration).

The most obvious route to take with this question would be to describe a study of language training in primates. Savage-Rumbaugh's or Premack's research would provide equally rich sources of material. An equally valid approach would be to critically consider comparative studies of, for example, birdsong, bee dances or cetacean communication.

3   BIO-PSYCHOLOGY

Question 1

Outline answer for the autonomic nervous system (ANS)

(a) Describe ANS structure and function:

1   Brain:
- Structures: hypothalamus and limbic system.
- Functions: regulates ANS via autonomic nuclei in the brainstem.

2   Sympathetic branch of ANS:
- Structure: sympathetic nerves lie slightly outside spinal cord, connected to involuntary organs such as the heart, stomach and liver.
- Function: to activate internal organs for activity directly through nerves or indirectly through the hormonal system.

3   Parasympathetic branch:
- Structure: parasympathetic nerves connected to same organs; originate also outside spinal cord but at the top and bottom (cranial and sacral sections).
- Function: to conserve energy and monitor relaxed state of organism.

(b) Assess the effects of the ANS on:

1   Physiological functions:
- Sympathetic branch of ANS: e.g. heart rate increased, sugar released from liver, pupils dilated, and production of saliva and digestive processes inhibited.
- Parasympathetic branch: e.g. slows heart rate, stores sugar, and stimulates saliva and digestive processes.
- Hormones produced because hypothalamus stimulates endocrine system, most importantly the adrenal gland which produces adrenalin (epinephrine) for arousal or noradrenalin for the inverse state.

2   Behavioural functions: homeostatic control of hunger, thirst and temperature. Also emotions, stress, motivation, sleep and arousal.

Outline answer for the endocrine system

(a) Description of endocrine system structure and function should include:

1   Brain:
- Structure: hypothalamus connects to pituitary gland.
- Function: produces hormones and controls endocrine glands.

2 Endocrine glands:

- Structure: ductless glands (exocrine system glands have ducts, e.g. saliva glands).

- Function: passes hormones directly into the blood. Main examples are adrenal, thyroid and pancreatic glands and the gonads.

(b) Assess the effects of the endocrine system on:

1 Physiological functions: hormones regulate growth, reproductive functions, water balance. Their effects are slower than the nervous system, only affect target organs.

2 Behavioural functions: as for ANS.

Examiner's tip A good answer should be balanced, offering material for parts (a) and (b), and covering both behavioural and physiological functions. Candidates who discuss the effects of only one function will receive a maximum of 8 marks, and those who write about the nervous system generally are unlikely to attract many marks at all because of the lack of selectivity.

Candidates who write about both the ANS and endocrine system will only be credited for one though there is considerable overlap between the systems.

Question 2

Examiner's tip There are a number of critical words in this question. First, the injunction to 'discuss' warns that you should present both description (Skill A) and evaluation (Skill B). The second important word is 'research' which refers to theoretical as well as empirical accounts (see glossary of key words in the Introduction). Therefore you might describe studies or theories (Skill A) and then, if you described studies, use theories as a means of evaluation (Skill B) or, if you described theories, use studies as the means of evaluation. Third, you should note that your discussion must be limited to the cerebral cortex and exclude sub-cortical structures. Finally, beware of discussing animal research which will receive no credit because the question asks for the 'human cerebral cortex'.

Before you attempt the question make sure that you know the difference between localization and lateralization.

The concept 'localization' refers to the fact that many behaviours are consistently associated with specific areas of the cortex. One of the best known is language, which is both localized and lateralized. Lateralized means that the function is located in only one hemisphere. Localized means that the function is located in a specific area. In most people the language centres are lateralized on the left side of the brain and localized in specific areas, notably Broca and Wernicke's areas.

Broca's area was named after the surgeon who first identified it in the nineteenth century. He came across a number of patients who had trouble speaking but could understand language perfectly. He was able to examine their brains when they died and found that they all had damage to the anterior frontal lobe of the left cerebral cortex. Subsequent research has shown that people who have damage to this area of the brain have slow, poorly articulated speech and some difficulties with comprehension. It has also been shown that when people speak there is increased blood flow to Broca's area.

Also in the nineteenth century, Wernicke found a number of patients with a different kind of language difficulty; they could produce grammatical speech but were not able to comprehend what others were saying. He found that their brains showed damage to the posterior left temporal area. Therefore this area is associated with speech production and comprehension.

Split brain studies such as those conducted by Sperry (1968) showed how patients with no connection between the left (language) hemisphere and right (controls left hand) hemisphere could not say the name of something they were holding in their left hand. The same was true if the subjects were shown an object to their left visual field (which goes to the right hemisphere from both eyes). Patients did learn some strategies for dealing with this. If they said the wrong answer (hearing is bilateral) they could hear it was wrong and would frown. The left hemisphere, sensing the frown would realize the answer was wrong and try again.

However, language is not always located in the left hemisphere. In some people it is found in the same area in the right hemisphere or in both hemispheres (bilateral), in which case it is localized but not lateralized. Most left-handers have been found to have bilateral language centres. The evidence for this comes from the fact that damage to either hemisphere results in impaired language. Left-handers have to control their writing hand with the opposite hemisphere because the left hand will be controlled by the right hemisphere (a lateralized function). This may explain why some left-handers use a strange inverted writing posture.

> **Examiner's tip** Note that this is an application of the research described, a good way to gain Skill B credit. In fact applications can be Skill A (accurate description/knowledge) but they are Skill B when used in an evaluative sense, such as demonstrating the usefulness of some research or theory (as here).

The problem of dyslexia has been linked to language localization. There are two kinds of dyslexia: children who are born with the problem have developmental dyslexia, the other kind is called acquired dyslexia and is the result of a specific brain injury. All dyslexics have difficulty with reading, writing and spelling but this appears in many different forms. For example, some dyslexics have speech disorders whereas others have problems with visual perception (confusing the letters b and d). The different kinds of dyslexia may depend on the specific area where damage has occurred. It may also be that some dyslexics have bilateral language centres and this leads to linguistic confusion such as the letter reversals.

Other research has found that stuttering may be related to lack of lateralization. Jones (1966) had to operate on patients who had brain tumours near their speech centres. Normally he might not have operated but in these patients he established that they all had speech centres on both the right and left by using sodium amytal to paralyse the left side and observing that they could still talk. These patients all stuttered and their stuttering stopped after the operation. Other research has found that more stutterers than non-stutterers have mixed or right-hand dominance for speech.

As can be seen, much of this evidence is based on observations of people with brain damage, either from behavioural observations or post-mortem examinations linked with known behaviours. Evidence from brain damaged patients can be criticized for a number of reasons. First of all, it is not possible to make before and after comparisons and therefore you cannot be certain that the injury is what caused the person to have the problem or whether they had some difficulty prior to the injury. Second, you cannot be sure that a primary cause has been located: if you have your vocal chords removed you cannot speak but that does not mean that they are where the brain's language centres are located. Third, the fact that a

person has had a traumatic injury may be the reason for their changed behaviour rather than any specific damage. Finally, studies of brain damage tend to be case studies involving very small if not unique samples. Therefore it may not be realistic to generalize from them. In the case of split-brain patients, they all were epileptics and had abnormal brains anyway.

| Examiner's tip | The candidate is critically evaluating the research evidence. |

Unless the brain has been examined in a post-mortem you also do not know the specific location of the damage. In fact a large area may have been affected and therefore it is not possible to say which of the damaged bits was responsible for the behaviour affected. More recent methods such as EEG and X-ray tomography mean that the brain activity can be examined in normal and abnormal people and related to current behaviour. Another method which does not involve damage to the patient is using temporary paralysis to one hemisphere by injecting the drug sodium amytal. Alternatively researchers can stimulate parts of the brain with electrodes and ask a subject to report the sensations.

Are there any applications of this research? When people suffer strokes which result in the loss of certain functions because specific areas have been damaged, it is helpful to know how likely they are to recover. Research on brain localization indicates that even adult brains have some plasticity. The younger you are the more the brain is capable of growth; this is called the Kennard principle (Kennard, 1938). Some functions are easier to transfer to other areas of the brain but language appears to be tied to very localized areas from birth. Ethologists have used the concept of critical or sensitive periods to describe the fact that there are windows in development when the organism is maximally sensitive to certain things. If development does not occur within this window it may not happen at all. Studies of children who have failed to acquire language before a certain age indicate that after puberty it is no longer possible to develop the ability to use grammar. The study of Genie (Curtiss, 1977) showed this and so did the study by Singleton and Newport (1993) of a deaf boy called Simon. Simon's parents could communicate using ASL but not grammatically because they only learned it after puberty. However, Simon developed grammatical ASL just from seeing his parents sign.

Therefore it is thought that language centres will atrophy after a certain age if not used. Other research has found that children with brain damage in these areas will be able to overcome this by utilizing other areas of the brain, such as the right side. But this plasticity disappears in adulthood. Language is one of the functions that is highly specialized, reflecting the fact that it only exists in humans and possibly higher mammals.

| Examiner's tip | This is good use of material from other areas of the psychology syllabus, namely language acquisition. Such research clearly relates to the development of localized (and lateralized) functions and therefore is relevant and good evidence of placing the answer in a wider context. |

Finally we might ask why there would be any evolutionary advantage to having some behaviours localized in the cortex? It would seem that lateralization may prevent speech confusions which would occur if there were two competing speech centres. Specialization has the disadvantage that any individual who suffers damage to a particular area may lose that function but it has the advantage of offering the species certain innate potentials.

Examiner's tip The strengths of this answer lie in the well-detailed and accurate material presented at the beginning as to the various specialized language centres. The section evaluating methodology is very clear and good evidence for Skill B. There are many other attempts to include Skill B material, such as looking at applications and seeking to find some reason for cortical localization. Knowledge and coherence are strong.

The approach here has been to look at one example (language) in depth. You could equally tackle the question in breadth by describing the various aspects of behaviour which are localized in the cortex (e.g. sensory and motor cortical control, vision, hearing, memory, language and thought, but not motivation and emotion because these are sub-cortical) and presenting some research relevant to each. You could then evaluate each as you go along or, as was done here, present a block of methodological and other considerations.

Question 3

Examiner's tip The 'compare and contrast' essay is a classic. It is a way of asking for descriptions and evaluations, the latter by setting the competing explanations against each other. In comparing various explanations you should identify differences, but you must also discuss how they are similar.

Despite the simplicity of such questions, examiner's reports repeatedly say that candidates fail to address the 'compare and contrast' part. This may reflect the fact that it is more difficult to do than it sounds and therefore only the most able candidates will be

There are a number of theories about why animals need sleep. In this essay I will describe and evaluate two rather different views: the restorative and evolutionary models, and then compare them with each other.

The repair and restoration (R&R) theory proposes that sleep enables the individual to recover both physically and psychologically. Intuitively people feel that this is the purpose of sleep, they say that they 'feel better after a good night's sleep'. There is physiological evidence to support this view. During slow wave sleep the body has time to make repairs, such as removing waste products and replenishing the supply of synaptic transmitters. Certain metabolic processes also increase at night, for example, there is increased production of growth hormone and increased protein synthesis, particularly in REM sleep.

Psychological repair is one of the suggested reasons for dreams. During REM sleep, it may be that, for example, memory is consolidated and dreams serve to sift through personal experiences. Evans (1984) described dreams using computer analogies. He suggested that they enable us to update memory files, discard redundant data, rehearse and check mental routines. However, McCarley's (1983) activation-synthesis model suggests that dreams are the subjective experience of nonsensical spontaneous neural activity during sleep.

If repair and restoration was the only function of sleep we would expect to observe that sleep deprivation has detrimental effects and that increased sleep followed great physical exertion. One of the classic pieces of research was done by Jouvet (1967) using the flowerpot technique. He placed a cat on a platform just large enough to hold it, surrounded by water. During slow wave sleep the animal snoozes, but in REM sleep the loss of muscle tone causes it to slip off. The cat soon learns to awaken when its head begins to nod and therefore goes without REM sleep. He found that his subjects behaved strangely and eventually died.

Examiner's tip This is a good way to approach evaluation, asking what we would expect to be the case if our theory is true.

Certain case studies of humans have also found some severe effects from sleep deprivation but this is not a universal finding. For example, a disc jockey, Peter Tripp, stayed awake for 200 hours as a publicity stunt. He developed severe paranoid psychosis with the delusion that he was being poisoned. This was reported by Dement who reported another case, of a 17-year-old (Randy Gardner) who stayed awake for 264 hours. He suffered some blurred vision, incoherent speech and some mild paranoia but only slept for 15 hours at the end of it. Dement also, in a study of eight volunteers, found that REM deprivation for more than a week only resulted in mild temporary behavioural changes. Horne and Minard (1985) tried to exhaust their subjects with numerous activities and found that they went to sleep faster but not for longer.

The question is whether people need specific elements of sleep or whether it is all serving a repair function. The fact that people can cope with some deprivation and that they never make up the exact amount of sleep they have lost suggests that it is not all necessary. Horne says that sleep deprived subjects often have more stage 3 and 4 and REM sleep (REM rebound) on subsequent nights. He calls this 'core sleep' and suggests that it is only this sleep which is truly essential and has to be made up. Horne also suggests that some recovery can take place during relaxed wakefulness.

The evolutionary theory explains sleep as an adaptive response to environmental and internal demands, a bit like hibernation. Animals have evolved an innate programme (sleep) which protects them at times of danger, protects them from excessive wear and tear, and enables them to conserve energy because during sleep their metabolic requirements are reduced. When we talk of an animal 'evolving' something, this does not mean that they have deliberately chosen this behaviour but that the behaviour has been naturally selected because it makes the animal 'fitter'.

Examiner's tip This displays a good understanding of evolutionary concepts, the 'wider context'.

If adaptive value was the <u>only</u> function of sleep we would expect that there should be an inverse relationship between the time needed to search for food and the time needed for sleep. This is true for cows, who graze almost all the time and sleep little, and cats, who eat rapidly and sleep a lot. It would also follow from an evolutionary theory of sleep that animals likely to be attacked will sleep little and lightly. This is also largely true – predators do sleep more than animals who are preyed upon, and animals who are preyed upon often sleep in burrows and feed at night, such as rabbits. But taken to its logical conclusion it means that some animals should not sleep at all to ensure their safety; the fact that all animals sleep means that that there must be another purpose for sleep. Similarly a species who lives in an environment with no day or night (such as deep sea fish) should not sleep with any regularity. Not much is known about sleep in fish.

How can we compare and contrast these two theories? The two theories are not mutually exclusive. It is easy to see how the repair and restorative function of sleep might have evolved, but aspects of evolutionary theory are very different in suggesting that sleep is a means of reducing demands on the animal whereas R&R theory suggests that sleep is a time to recharge your batteries.

Examiner's tip Do not waste time in an examination repeatedly writing out the phrase 'repair and restoration' when R&R will be perfectly clear to the examiner. In general, you should write out the full phrase first, abbreviate and then use the abbreviation subsequently.

Neither theory adequately accounts for why animals have to lose consciousness when sleeping. It is not necessary for repair and restoration; Horne suggested that some physical repair could occur during a state of relaxed wakefulness. From a safety (adaptive) point of view loss of consciousness makes little sense.

Both theories have been used to explain why infants sleep more than older children. Evolutionary theory suggests that increased sleep has evolved as a means of helping exhausted parents to cope with finding food and other things. The R&R view suggests that infancy is a time of enormous brain and body growth and learning, therefore the infant needs extra time for recovery and consolidation.

The solution may lie in a combined view that sleep performs different functions in different species and at different times. The fact that different species evolve different sleep habits suggests that they all need sleep physiologically but the way it is achieved has to be adapted to their particular style of life. As we saw earlier, grazing animals sleep less because they have to have more time to eat. Dolphins sleep one hemisphere at a time which may be related to the fact that if they lose consciousness entirely they will drown because they have to surface regularly to breathe. In winter, and when animals are young, increased sleep might be related to metabolic requirements.

Examiner's tip The final part of this essay attempts to address the 'compare and contrast', lifting a competent essay into the top band because it answers the question which was set rather than just presenting excellent but prepared material on theories of sleep. This essay is well-structured and uses empirical evidence effectively though some might be cited more exactly.

Sleep is a popular topic, and therefore many candidates answer the question by writing down everything they know about it. Any description of sleep and dream stages will attract almost no marks in relation to this question. The same is true of an answer that describes more than two theories, unless they are used as a means of evaluating one of your chosen theories.

Question 4

Examiner's tip In this question Skill A will be an explanation of the issues in relation to theories, and Skill B will evaluate these explanations using theoretical and empirical evidence.

Beware that the question asks for 'physiological factors in emotion' therefore cognitive theories will only be relevant by way of contrast (as a means of evaluation). Also beware that the question does not ask for a list of physiological factors but for the role such factors play.

It is quite tempting to read the question and then produce a standard essay on theories of emotion and this will be the most common response. If you wish to obtain a high mark you must demonstrate that you are answering this question rather than one entitled

There are three theories which describe how changes in the brain relate to emotion. They are called the James–Lange, Cannon–Bard and Schachter's cognitive labelling theories. Each of them describes how physiological (bodily states) and psychological factors contribute to the experience of emotion.

In the nineteenth century James and Lange both said that physiological arousal comes first and this forms the basis of an emotional experience. You are frightened when you see a bear because you run, rather than feeling frightened and therefore running away. This is the opposite of the common-sense view of emotional experience.

Cannon (1927) criticized the James–Lange view and put forward his own, which was modified by Bard. The Cannon–Bard theory is that physiological changes in the autonomic nervous system (ANS) and subjective experience occur simultaneously and independently and are of equal importance. The Cannon–Bard criticisms of the

James–Lange theory are that there would have to be different physiological states for each emotional experience, that physiological changes do not necessarily produce emotional states, that emotional states can occur without any physiological changes, and that emotional experiences occur quite rapidly whereas the ANS is relatively slow to respond.

The third theory was proposed by Schachter. He said that all emotional experiences are preceded by a state of general ANS arousal, but the nature of the subjective experience is determined by the individual's cognitive assessment, not by any differences in physiological state. Cognitions may come from external, situational cues or internal ones such as imagination. Like the James–Lange view, this suggests that emotion is based on arousal, however cognitive labelling theory proposes that there is just one physiological state which is labelled according to situational cues. When a person feels aroused their mind seeks an explanation, and past experience or situational cues provide a label.

In order to decide which view is right psychologists have looked at empirical studies. There is evidence which supports the James–Lange theory. Cannon and many other psychologists thought that there were not different physiological states but more recent evidence shows that there are. Schwartz *et al.* (1981) asked subjects to close their eyes and imagine certain situations which would make them feel happy, sad, angry or afraid. The researchers measured the subjects' heart rate and blood pressure and found that each emotion produced a different physiological 'signature'. Ekman *et al.* (1983) also found physiological signatures when they asked subjects to show various facial expressions for different emotions. Laird (1974) told subjects that he was measuring activity of facial muscles using electrodes and instructed them to relax and contract muscles. He found that cartoons viewed when 'smiling' were rated as funnier. Subjects were amused because they were smiling, not smiling because they were amused. These studies support James' view but also show that this is not the only explanation. Schwartz's study also supports the opposite view because their subjects were asked to have a subjective experience and this led to physiological arousal.

There is other evidence that demonstrates that you do not have to be aroused at all to experience emotion. Valins (1966) showed his subjects some slides of attractive women while he tested their physiological reactions. The subjects actually were given false feedback so that during some slides it sounded as if their heart was beating faster than during other slides. Valins found that when subjects thought they were aroused (faster heartbeats) they rated those pictures as more attractive. This evidence supports Cannon's views in two ways. Subjects had emotional states without actual physiological arousal, and subjects were obviously not aware of their own physiological state otherwise they would not have believed the false feedback. Hohmann (1966) found the same thing when he interviewed patients with spinal cord injuries. They said they still experienced emotion though they had almost no physiological sensations.

The reverse is also true: you can have physiological arousal but experience no emotions. Marañon (1924) injected patients with adrenalin and asked them to report what they experienced; most of them reported the physical sensations with no emotional overtones. The fact that this study relies on introspection means that we should treat the results cautiously. It is also very old and from a foreign journal, which means that no one reads the original. Schachter and Singer (1962) also injected subjects with adrenalin (the subjects thought it was a new vitamin). They told some of the subjects that the vitamin would make them feel aroused; other subjects were not told of any side effects. The subjects were placed in a room with a confederate who was either very happy or very angry. If subjects were expecting to feel aroused they were not very affected by the confederate's behaviour. Those subjects who had not been told what they might experience mimicked the confederate's behaviour. The researchers explained this as being due to the fact that the uninformed subjects were experiencing a state of arousal but had no explanation for it so they sought to label it using situational cues. The informed subjects had an explanation for what they felt. It is worth noting that there have been criticisms of this study, namely that other psychologists have had difficulty replicating it. Also it is important that Schachter and Singer excluded some subjects from the final analysis because the subjects guessed the purpose of the experiment. The results were not significant without getting rid of these subjects.

> **Examiner's tip** The full details of this classic study have not been reported here. The candidate has done well to be selective, including only the relevant details.

James's theory also predicts that the more intense the arousal the greater the emotion because if subjective emotion is based on arousal, then the strength of the experience should be related to the strength of arousal. White *et al.* (1981) asked male students to run on the spot and then showed them videos of some women they would meet later. Those who ran for 2 minutes found the videos of <u>attractive</u> women more attractive than those who ran for only 15 seconds, whereas the opposite was true if the woman was unattractive. This suggests that arousal enhances existing emotional states.

You can also have an emotional response with no cognitive awareness. McGinnies (1949) showed that subjects produced a galvanic skin response (GSR) when exposed to taboo words for a very short duration, so short that they were unable to recognize the words. A GSR indicates autonomic arousal and therefore shows that they experienced arousal with no cognitive awareness.

It would seem that no view is entirely correct. Physiological arousal alone can be sufficient but it is not always necessary or first. This might be related to different kinds of emotional experience. Some are more physiological than others; for example; when you hear a loud noise your body reacts by becoming aroused and this may lead you to feel afraid or excited. Other emotional experiences are more cognitive, such as hearing that you passed your exams. This makes you feel good which in turn may cause a physiological sensation.

Therefore we can see that physiological factors do play a role in emotion but they are not always necessary or first.

> **Examiner's tip** This is a very competent essay on theories of emotion, using empirical evidence in a highly structured and relatively critical manner. There are attempts to bend the answer towards the question especially as the last sentence reflects some of the words used in the quotation.
>
> A different approach might have been to describe the brain structures concerned with emotion and discuss how these relate to physiological changes and emotional experience, using theories to evaluate the account you present.
>
> Candidates who manage to avoid referring to the quotation may only earn a maximum of 20 marks. One approach would be to begin the essay by paraphrasing the quotation and then you can be sure you have addressed it, or you can incorporate the quotation in full in the context of answering the question.
>
> Listing physiological changes will probably only receive low band marks unless the candidate has discussed the role of these changes.

4   ATYPICAL DEVELOPMENT AND ABNORMAL BEHAVIOUR

Question 1

Examiner's tip This question does not require a description of the actual disabilities but of their psychological effects. You might organise your answer either in terms of different physical and sensory disabilities, describing the psychological effects of each (Skill A) followed by appropriate evaluative comments (Skill B). Or you might organise the essay in terms of psychological effects, many of which are common to more than one disability, such as the effects on cognitive and social development. This is the approach taken here. As a starting point you could write down all the possible psychological effects and use this as the backbone of your essay.

Beware of giving an anecdotal account containing little psychology. Many candidates may have personal experiences of certain disabilities and are tempted to base their essays on these experiences. Such accounts are unlikely to receive much credit because they will not be 'psychologically-informed'.

Children who have physical disabilities, such as visual and hearing disability, or cerebral palsy, have many associated physical and sensory disabilities. Some of these are the direct result of their disability while others arise indirectly. In this essay I will examine various psychological effects and relate these to particular disabilities, I will evaluate these effects in terms of how critical the disability is in the child's development and what can be done to help the child.

Examiner's tip It is useful to start the essay by making the structure explicit, thus helping the examiner to know where to look.

One of the most important effects of disabilities is on cognitive development. Children who have Down's syndrome are mentally retarded which obviously affects their cognitive development. They reach the same milestones as normal children, such as speaking, but much later. The degree of retardation varies enormously and is related to other factors such as what additional disabilities they may have and the amount of stimulation they get at home.

Both visual and hearing impairment may indirectly affect cognitive development because the sensory defect interferes with learning. Phelps and Branyan (1990) found that non-verbal IQ scores for pre-linguistically deaf children are consistently one standard deviation or more below normal. Deaf children have difficulty reading because reading is taught through saying words out loud and such reading deficits slow down their cognitive development. Blind children have to learn to use Braille which is a poor substitute for reading because it has a smaller visual field, places greater demand on short-term memory, is harder to learn and slower to process.

Children with such difficulties may be helped by language training and special education programmes in school. There is a continuing argument over whether they are better served in separate schools or within mainstream education. For social reasons, children who can function in a normal classroom probably should be placed there because it helps them adjust to normal life and helps other children to understand better the problems of disability and to hold less stereotyped views of retardation.

This is especially true because the social development as well as the cognitive development of disabled children is often affected by their disabilities. First of all, they may have difficulty with communication, particularly language and nonverbal behaviour, which affects their ability to interact socially (as well as their cognitive development). Using sign language as a form of communication is becoming increasingly widespread. However, the deaf will always find social interactions difficult and deaf children's emotional and social development will be hampered by this. Secondly, a young visually impaired child may suffer emotionally because smiling is important for attachment. Lack of visual contact continues to disable such children in social encounters.

Down's syndrome children are noted for their friendliness, cheerfulness and sociability which appear to be behavioural traits linked to the condition.

Examiner's tip This detail about Down's syndrome is bordering on the anecdotal. However, it is a common observation in textbooks and indicates that the candidate is 'well-informed' about Down's syndrome. It also is an attempt to show that some effects of disability can be positive.

Another aspect of development which is affected by disability is motor development. Visually impaired children have problems with the development of sensorimotor co-ordination because they do not get appropriate visual feedback when they use their arms and legs. They also cannot see where they are going. There is evidence that their other senses become more sensitive to compensate for their lack of vision.

Cerebral palsy is a motor disability where individuals have difficulty controlling the muscles of their arms, legs and/or head. Therefore this disability directly affects motor development. The condition is due to brain cell death in the motor cortex usually caused by a lack of oxygen (anoxia). This may happen before or during birth, or it can happen later in infancy. Quite often such children have brain damage to other areas of the brain, such as the visual or auditory cortex, so that they often have multiple disabilities. Mild anoxia may cause minimal brain damage which often goes undiagnosed, and the child is simply regarded as clumsy and intellectually below average.

Disability also may lead to behavioural problems. First of all, being 'sick' requires psychological adjustment. Some children find this difficult, for example, a child diagnosed as diabetic may rebel against the major changes which are required to their lifestyle such as having a carefully regulated diet, daily injections and glucose monitoring. Their anger may be expressed in various ways such as becoming withdrawn or aggressive as a means of expressing their anger (acting out).

Second, handicapped children may have a negative self-image and low self-esteem which means they are more prone to failure. This self-image is based on the negative reactions of others, and disabled children learn to dislike themselves. Parents invariably are upset and depressed by the birth of a disabled baby and before they learn to accept the problem their feelings are communicated to their child. Disabled children have far less access to role models with whom they can identify. For some disabled, it is not clear whether they belong to the 'disabled' or the 'normal' population, and this further confuses their sense of identity. Cowen and Bobrove (1966) found that the totally disabled were better adjusted than those who had partial disabilities, presumably because their group identity was clearer.

One way to help improve self-image is to place disabled children in mainstream education, although then disabled children may also experience a greater sense of what they cannot do and of rejection.

Labelling may have a positive or a negative effect on self-image. A label is a word or phrase which represents a number of other characteristics. Labels lead to expectations which have a self-fulfilling effect. If the expectations are that disabled people will not be able to do things then the label perpetuates the expectation and makes it hard for the image to change. Perhaps for this reason people keep changing the labels for disabilities, for example, saying 'hearing impairment' rather

than 'deafness'. On the other hand a label may help a disabled child receive appropriate treatment or education. Labels may also be a means of preventing a child being accused of laziness or stupidity as in the case of children who have difficulty with reading; when dyslexia is diagnosed they can be taught properly and not regarded as stupid.

Finally we should consider the effects of disabilities on parents and carers. They also have to adjust to the experience of having a disabled child which could lower their self-esteem and undoubtedly changes their lives. In some families, certain disabilities are less of a problem. For example, a sport-oriented family would find it more difficult to adjust to a child with physical disabilities whereas an academic family might find a mentally retarded child more difficult. Similarly, disabilities are more of a disadvantage in fast-moving, urban settings than in a rural community.

Examiner's tip Some candidates may find this a difficult question partly because the topic is not dealt with very well in popular textbooks. However, a good candidate can work out what effects disability might have (e.g. on cognitive, social, motor and personal development) and 'hang' their knowledge on this framework.

The answer given here may contain little specific evidence but covers a wide range of developmental issues. These are indeed evaluated rather than just described because evidence is offered to qualify the points, such as suggesting how low self-esteem might be improved. The answer is coherent, and accurate, and conveys psychological understanding, as in the case of cerebral palsy and the effects of expectations on self-image. The candidate's knowledge has been used to good effect in answering the question.

Question 2

Examiner's tip For Skill A you must describe the medical model. For Skill B you should evaluate this model through direct criticisms and by presenting alternative models as a contrast. Criticisms may be in terms of classification, diagnosis, side effects, treatments and ethics. You do not need to take sides but must present a reasoned argument and relevant empirical evidence.

The medical model is based on the assumption that all mental illnesses have a biological cause. It does not mean that the cause is known. The medical model also involves the idea that a diagnosis can be made through observing signs and symptoms. Then the appropriate course of treatment can be applied, taking key variables into account such as the patient's history and age. Another aspect of the medical model is that it promotes the idea that causes can be found and therefore psychologists conduct research into genetic or neurological causes.

Examiner's tip This is a sound description of the medical model, covering its assumptions and effects.

There is some support for this model. A number of psychological disorders have been shown to have a biological cause. For example, in the sixteenth century there was a mental illness called general paresis. It was eventually realized that the cause was syphilis. In order to connect the symptoms with the cause it was necessary to first be able to describe the symptoms of the illness. This meant that a number of people who had the same disease could be identified and eventually a cause was traced.

A different example of a biological cause is an inherited condition. There is evidence that some mental illnesses have a genetic basis. For example, Kendler (1983) found that monozygotic twins were much more likely than dizygotic twins to both have schizophrenia. A more recent explanation for schizophrenia is that the cause is a retrovirus which has been inherited. This is also a genetic explanation.

Biological causes also include neurochemical explanations, such as the proposal that schizophrenia is linked with excess dopamine. This is based on the fact that certain drugs, for example LSD or L-dopa, induce schizophrenic-like states. It is known that these drugs increase dopamine levels and it is also known that L-dopa aggravates the symptoms of schizophrenics. This has led schizophrenics to be treated successfully with drugs to block dopamine production. Other illnesses are also successfully treated with drugs, for example, antidepressants are used with people suffering from depression. These drugs affect noradrenalin levels and therefore it might be that depression is linked to noradrenalin in some way.

The problem with neurochemical explanations is that such chemicals may be either a cause or an effect of the illness. They may be due to some genetic abnormality or they may be produced by certain mental states, as is the case when a state of anxiety (psychological cause) leads to a release of adrenalin.

Evidence for the medical model also comes from cases where individuals have suffered some brain injury, illness or tumour and they exhibit psychological symptoms. For example, some amnesias are due to brain damage to specific areas. Excess alcohol sometimes causes significant brain damage leading to Korsakoff's syndrome, a condition where patients experience memory disturbances, confusion and apathy.

The evidence demonstrates that <u>some</u> abnormality arises because of known biological causes. However, the assumption that all abnormality is due to illness may be mistaken and dangerous. The alternative view is that abnormality in fact is something which society regards as unusual or dangerous. Szasz (1960) criticized the medical model as being misleading because it prevents us investigating the true problems. He said that the medical model promotes the idea of the doctor as all powerful and it removes personal responsibility. The medical approach was an attempt to move away from the nineteenth century view that the patient was at fault for their illness but Szasz suggests that the medical model replaces one kind of demonology with a different means of social control. These are ethical criticisms of the medical model because they suggest that the medical model means that one group of people are allowed to make decisions of what is desirable and undesirable in others.

Laing (1965) said that insanity was a normal response to an abnormal world. He pointed out that it is usually society rather than the patient who is disturbed by abnormal behaviour. Therefore we should realize that the diagnosis of madness is a question of who is doing the diagnosing. The medical model gives the illusion of objectivity.

We should look at practical considerations too. The medical model is only valuable if diagnoses are reliable, valid and provide effective and appropriate treatment. Cooper *et al.* (1972) found that American psychiatrists were much more likely to diagnose schizophrenia than their British counterparts, which suggests that their diagnoses were unreliable and based on their viewpoint rather than an objective state of affairs.

Diagnoses should be valid. Heather (1976) claimed that the same diagnosis had a 50% chance of leading to the same or different treatment which suggests that diagnoses have little value.

The medical model may sometimes be inappropriate for even clearly physical illnesses because the same treatment is not always effective for everyone, and a straightforward consideration of symptoms may ignore other, psychological factors. However, Clare (1980) points out that all illnesses have a physical and a psychological component. In particular stress has a significant effect on susceptibility and recovery for all illness.

Are medical model treatments effective? Somatic treatments are most commonly linked with the medical model, especially the use of drugs. However, drugs treat physical illnesses by killing off a virus or bacteria; with mental illnesses they reduce the symptoms but do not cure the problem in the same way.

There are other approaches to the definition of abnormality. For example, a common idea is to think in terms of statistical frequency so that abnormality is defined by the frequency of a particular behaviour. Using this definition, it would be undesirable to be a genius and desirable to be divorced.

Another approach is to define abnormal behaviour in terms of deviance from certain social standards. The problem with this is that such standards are relative to prevailing views of what is acceptable and allow corrupt regimes to abuse individual rights. For example, dissidents in Russia were at one time locked up in mental asylums, as were homosexuals and unmarried mothers in this country.

Abnormality has also been defined in terms of mental health. Jahoda (1958) suggested a list of characteristics such as self-acceptance, autonomy, accurate perception of reality, competence and positive interpersonal relations. This has similarities with Rogers' view of self-acceptance as the means to mental health. However, these views are again related to prevailing attitudes and are probably too vague for the purpose of many psychological disorders and their treatment.

It can be seen from this that there are many advantages and disadvantages associated with the medical model of abnormality. Diagnosis can lead to identification of a cause or syndrome, and then effective treatment. On the other hand it may mean that true causes are overlooked.

Examiner's tip The most popular approach to this question will probably involve a description of three or four main approaches to defining abnormality and some evaluation of each. The answer provided here bends itself more to the actual question set and draws on more varied material. It is well-structured, describes the medical model competently and presents good supporting evidence rather than just being critical – candidates are often better at expressing the anti-psychiatry view than displaying accurate knowledge of the medical model. Excellent answers should reflect the complexities of the field and the importance of premises and underlying ideologies.

Question 3

Examiner's tip This is a popular question for both examiners and students. It appears repeatedly in exam papers and candidates have well prepared answers, though the biological side is usually better understood than the environmental influences, and description is usually better done than evaluation. Therefore you must present something exceptional in order to attract the highest marks.

Part (a) requires Skill A only, a description of the symptoms to demonstrate your knowledge of the condition. Part (b) requires both Skills A and B. Note that the question specifically asks for 'evidence' and for both biological and environmental influences. A good answer will look at the interaction between these influences.

Outline answer for part (a)

You could include: multiple delusions, disordered thought (such as being controlled by aliens), hallucinations, blunting of emotional responses and motivation, lack of self identity, difficulties in planning and carrying out actions, and impairment of reality testing.

Examiner's tip Each symptom would be worth a notional 1 mark, however if you provided some more detail for some of the symptoms you might receive the full 4 marks for three symptoms only. It is important that you list symptoms which are exclusive to schizophrenia, and avoid presenting old stereotypes of schizophrenia, such as 'split personality', which would display a lack of detailed knowledge.

Outline answer for part (b)

1   Biological influences can include evidence from:

- *Genetic sources*: family studies e.g. Rosenthal (1970), twin studies e.g. Kendler (1983), adoption studies e.g. Wender *et al.* (1974), a retrovirus e.g. Crow (1984).

- *Neuroanatomical sources*: e.g. post-mortem examinations, PET and CAT scans show structural differences between brains of normal and schizophrenic people.

- *Neurochemical sources*: link with an excess of dopamine activity, either as a cause or an effect. Use studies related to how drugs have been shown to reduce or induce a psychotic state. Also post-mortem studies on levels of dopamine.

- *Known organic disorders*: such as brain tumours, which lead to psychotic states.

2   Environmental influences can include evidence from:

- *Schizophrenic families*: double-bind theory from Bateson (1956), the 'divided self' view from Laing (1959).

- *Social causes*: schizophrenia affects the poor more than the rich, either because the illness has caused persons to sink to low socio-economic status (social drift) or because the socio-economic disadvantages of the lower classes cause schizophrenia (social cause). Evidence from e.g. Turner and Wagenfeld (1967).

- *Environmental triggers*: stress may aggravate a tendency towards schizophrenia. Rabkin (1980) found no evidence for stress as a trigger.

3   An interaction between biological and environmental factors: *The diathesis-stress model*. 'Diathesis' is the susceptibility for an illness and 'stress' is the psychological reaction to meaningful events. The more susceptible you are the less stress will be required to trigger the symptoms. Schizophrenia occurs in biologically susceptible individuals who are exposed to disadvantageous environmental factors.

Examiner's tip Note the reliance on evidence as requested in the question. Your answer should present a balanced view, representing evidence for both kinds of influence as well as the possibility of an interaction of the two. The arguments and evidence should be described (Skill A) and evaluated (Skill B) in terms of conflicting research, methodological and/or ethical issues.

If only one influence is presented then there would be a maximum of 9 marks.

Question 4

Part (a) is clearly Skill A only, a description of somatic treatments. It will be tempting to stray into an evaluation of such methods but this would not receive any credit even in part (b), and will waste valuable time. Before choosing this question, make sure you know what 'somatic treatments' are; some students write about irrelevant therapies.

Part (b) involves both Skill A and Skill B, requiring you to discuss (i.e. name and evaluate) the difficulties in evaluating somatic treatments (i.e. not all therapies). This does not mean evaluating the treatments themselves but the difficulties in doing such evaluation. This is a common question and one that is often misinterpreted in the way described. You have been warned.

(a) The somatic approach to mental illness is one based on treating the body ('soma' means body). The three main treatments are ECT, psychosurgery and drug therapy.

ECT or electroconvulsive therapy involves administering an electric shock to a patient's brain, inducing a kind of epileptic fit. It was first introduced because some Italian psychologists noticed that epileptics never suffered from schizophrenia, therefore they reasoned that if you induced an epileptic fit in disturbed patients this might alleviate their symptoms. Originally insulin shock was used to create seizures.

Many people think of ECT as a barbaric kind of treatment and it used to involve much discomfort for the patient. Nowadays the patient is given an anaesthetic and muscle relaxant. An electric shock is applied to the nondominant cerebral hemisphere to produce a seizure. The individual awakens soon after and remembers nothing of the treatment. A course of treatment usually involves six sessions. It is one of the more successful treatments used in cases of severe depression. Fink (1978) concluded from a review of studies on ECT that it was effective in over 60% of psychotic-depressive patients using measures such as suicide rates.

No one knows why ECT works though there are various suggestions. It is possible that it acts as a form of punishment, or that the associated memory losses allow restructuring of disordered thinking. Alternatively a neurochemical explanation has been suggested – the shock causes a massive release of neurotransmitters such as serotonin which may help alleviate depression.

The evidence from Fink and the material on why ECT works is really Skill B and not relevant here. However, you would not lose marks by including it.

The second kind of somatic treatment is psychosurgery. This refers to any kind of brain surgery performed for the purpose of treating a psychological disorder. The best known example is lobotomy, first used by Moniz in the 1930s. He cut out large portions of a patient's frontal cerebral cortex in order to induce personality changes and make a patient more controllable. The results were quite variable. Such techniques are now used very rarely and only in cases of severe depression or pain where all other treatment has failed. The technique is also much refined, using electric probes which destroy specific nerve fibres and cause minimal intellectual damage.

Split-brain surgery is another example of psychosurgery where the two halves of the brain are separated to prevent severe epileptic fits. This was used by Sperry (1968).

The third form of somatic treatment is drug therapy, which has changed the treatment of mental illness considerably since it was first introduced in the 1950s. Many different kinds of drugs are used. Tranquillizers, such as Valium, are used to treat anxiety. It is now thought that these have been over-prescribed and there are many problems of addiction. Major tranquillizers, such as chlorpromazine, are used to treat psychotic conditions such as schizophrenia. The use of these drugs has meant that many mental patients no longer need to be kept in institutions because their psychological disturbance can be controlled. Antidepressant drugs, such as lithium, help manic depressives or people who are chronically depressed to lead relatively normal lives.

> **Examiner's tip** Some of the material offered here borders on the evaluative and an examiner might feel that this detracts from the quality of the answer because of some lack of selectivity – the candidate has written everything they know rather than what is relevant to the question. However, this must be considered in relation to the wealth of accurate, descriptive material which displays a high level of knowledge and understanding of somatic treatments.
>
> In general candidates find the topic of somatic treatment easy though they tend to focus on the horror stories of psychosurgery and ECT rather than displaying up-to-date familiarity with these methods.
>
> Candidates who describe one form of somatic treatment would receive a maximum of 6 marks because the question asks for treatment<u>s</u>.

(b) When psychologists try to evaluate the effectiveness of somatic treatments they experience certain difficulties.

The first problem lies with the concept of cure in relation to mental illness. The concept of a cure differs depending on the underlying assumptions of a particular approach. The medical model would accept alleviation of symptoms whereas the humanist approach would look for more general factors such as self-acceptance. The question must also be asked about how long-lasting the cure is; if the symptoms recur a year later can it be said that the patient was cured? In fact there is very little long-term follow-up research, therefore the available evidence only relates to immediate changes.

A second problem in evaluating effectiveness is deciding what measures are a valid means for assessment. The medical model is based on symptoms but some of these symptoms require the patient to report what they are feeling, for example when someone is depressed. The patient's self-report may be unreliable or suffer from the hello-goodbye effect. This is the tendency for patients to exaggerate how badly they were feeling at the beginning of treatment in order to convince their doctor or therapist that they are in genuine need. At the end of treatment, patients want to say they feel better as a means of expressing their thanks.

In some cases there may be objective means of assessing improvement by looking at target behaviours, such as asking a depressed patient to record how long they sleep, or using psychometric tests. But both of these presume that the patient will be honest. Furthermore the assessment of effectiveness depends on a reliable diagnosis in the first place.

Third, if there is apparent improvement we do not know that the treatment is responsible for the change in behaviour. Spontaneous remission is a possibility, in the case of depression particularly since time alone or changed home circumstances can lead to an improvement. Eysenck (1952) analysed a number of studies about the effectiveness of treatment and found that 66% of patients improved without any treatment. His study has been criticized by others, for example, if you exclude the patients who dropped out of psychoanalysis, then 66% of the patients who received treatment also improved. Smith et al. (1980) reviewed a very large number of studies which compared treated and untreated patients and concluded that a wide variety of therapies were all more effective than no therapy.

Letts
Q&A

> **Examiner's tip** This is a good use of empirical evidence to argue for and against a point. The details such as dates and percentages are not necessary for a high mark but do contribute to the essay's accuracy and detail.

All methods of treatment involve increased attention for a patient and therefore even patients undergoing somatic treatment may improve because of other factors such as their relationship with the doctor treating them rather than the target method of treatment.

It is also true that the expectations a patient has about the effectiveness of the treatment can affect its success, so that what appears to be a successful therapy is in fact due to their expectations.

Fourth is the problem of lack of control groups. The correct research procedure for evaluating a treatment would be to give it to one group and withhold it from another matched group. This can be done if waiting lists exist but it is still ethically questionable. Other ethical considerations involve patient confidentiality and the right of the patient to choose their therapy rather than being assigned to treatment groups. A proper evaluation of ECT would involve using patients who had not volunteered themselves for this treatment. The use of placebos is a possibility.

A fifth problem relates to the fact that different treatments are successful with different psychological disorders, which makes comparison and evaluation difficult. Kazdin (1986) found that behaviour therapy is the most effective means of treating phobias and that drug therapy is most successful with schizophrenic disorders and cognitive-behavioural methods are best with sexual problems. Therefore it would be unrepresentative to compare all three therapies in terms of treating phobias. Also, if we want to compare different therapeutic approaches it would be hard to agree on the same measure of assessment since they differ in their goals.

It can be seen that there are many difficulties in evaluating somatic therapies and providing comparisons with other methods or no treatment at all.

Examiner's tip A good answer should provide a good balance between description of the problems and evaluation. This answer manages to achieve this and to be coherent, appropriately selective and to cover the main issues.

If you only discuss one difficulty then there would be a maximum of 10 marks. Where a candidate criticizes somatic therapies rather than the difficulties of evaluation, there would be a maximum of 8 marks. No credit can be given for any difficulties which do not apply to somatic treatments.

---

5 COGNITIVE PSYCHOLOGY

Question 1

Examiner's tip Part questions, such as this one, are designed to help the candidate maximize their marks. The question could have been set as a single part essay: 'Describe and evaluate **one** theory of perception'. A good student would successfully break this single injunction down into constituent parts, such as first defining the key term(s), second describing one theory, and third evaluating this theory. The part question approach to question setting merely makes this breakdown explicit. It is there to help you, the candidate.

This question contains the rubric 'one theory'. If a candidate offers material on more than one theory, examiners can give no extra credit. However, they will select the theory which was best discussed. It might then seem to be a good strategy to write about more than one theory and let the examiner do the work for you, but this wastes considerable time. If you are really not sure which theory you know best, jot down a few notes about each and then decide. In part (c) you can use knowledge about other theories to help evaluate the first.

(a) Perception is the process of interpreting sensory data so that it has meaning. The eye records points of light but these are organized by the brain to produce information about, for example, depth or form. The eye records physical sensations but these are not very useful until they are organized into perceptions.

Examiner's tip There is a certain amount of repetitiveness in this definition but the candidate covers the key point (perception is different from sensation) and goes on to elaborate by way of some examples. It is often difficult to think of how to 'pad out' a definition for the marks shown and giving examples is a good strategy. We might say that the first sentence is worth 2 marks and the elaboration adds the remaining marks because of the understanding it conveys.

(b) Gregory's theory of perception is a top-down or constructivist theory. This theory is called 'top-down' because it starts in the brain rather than bottom-up which starts with the physical stimulus. Gregory did not mean that physical sensations do not play any part in the process, in fact he said that the perceptual process is like forming a hypothesis, which is first suggested and then tested by the sensory data. At the same time cognitive expectations influence the hypothesis from the beginning. When you look at something you have prior expectations which help you interpret the sensations recorded at your eye. The sensations are often incomplete or ambiguous and require some additional input in order to make sense.

Gregory used visual illusions to support his theory. The reason we see illusions is because the brain forms mistaken perceptions based on past experience and using cues from the sensory data. For example, in the Ponzo illusion one horizontal line looks longer than the other because the converging lines suggest perspective. The brain interprets the drawing on the basis of learned depth cues.

Top-down processes can also be seen in perceptual set. This is an expectation about what you think you will see, which influences what you finally perceive. For example, Bugelski and Alampay (1961) showed participants a series of drawings of either non-human animals or people, finishing with the ambiguous picture of the ratman. Participants were more likely to interpret the drawing as a rat if they had seen pictures of animals. This shows how past experience affects your cognitive expectations or perceptual set, which in turn affects what you perceive.

Examiner's tip This answer communicates a good understanding (Skill A) of Gregory's theory through the use of examples. It gains high marks partly because of its coherence, and also because it is well-detailed. One way of demonstrating detail is the precise citing and description of empirical evidence (e.g. Bugelski and Alampay, 1961). It is not compulsory to be able to refer to research exactly but it helps. If you are not sure you could say 'in the 1960s' or 'Bugelski and an assistant'.

(c) How does Gregory's theory help us to understand perceptual processes?

Examiner's tip It is sometimes helpful to start with the question itself just to remind you about the specific issues you are addressing. However, this should not be a knee-jerk reaction, introductions are by no means vital in an exam and may simply waste time.

I have already mentioned that Gregory's theory can explain visual illusions, such as the Ponzo illusion. Gregory also used it to explain the Müller–Lyer illusion in terms of mistaken depth perception. He thought the ingoing fins looked like the corner of a building and therefore it makes the vertical line seem closer. The outgoing fins are like the corner of a room and the vertical line appears farther away and therefore seems longer. However, if you put circles instead of fins on the end of the equal lines, the illusion is still apparent so Gregory's explanation cannot be right for all illusions. Segall *et al.* (1963) found that some African people do not see the Müller–Lyer illusion which supports

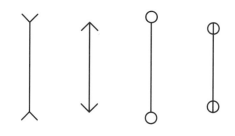

Gregory's idea that the illusion is the result of learned perceptions. It is suggested that people who live in carpentered environments learn these depth cues whereas people who live in round houses do not.

Gregory's theory also explains perceptual set as in the example of the ratman above. In another experiment (Bruner and Minturn) subjects were shown a set of numbers or a set of letters. In the middle appeared an ambiguous figure '13' Some subjects saw it as a 'B' and others saw it as a '13' depending on whether it was with letters or numbers. This shows how set influences what we perceive.

Examiner's tip Thus far the evaluation has been in terms of empirical support, looking at two different kinds of perceptual process, illusions and perceptual set. To some extent this is a repetition of material already credited in part (b), but it is elaborated and made relevant to this part of the question. If you do use material twice be sure to make it relevant to the question you are answering.

Gregory's theory can also be used to explain perceptual constancy. We learn to organize our sensory data in a way which makes sense. When looking at a book being moved around, the retinal image changes a lot yet we continue to perceive the same shape. This is called shape constancy. There is also colour, brightness and location constancy. All of these are based on our knowledge that certain things do not actually change even though the retinal image does.

However, Gregory's theory does not explain why vision is generally so accurate even in novel situations. An alternative view has been put forward by J.J. Gibson who believed that sensory data is an extremely rich source of information and perception can be explained solely in terms of bottom-up processes.

The Gestalt theory of perception also claimed that there are innate aspects of the way we build up meaningful perceptual units. For example, figure/ground organization is the way we see figures set against a background. Proximity is when things which occur together in space and time are 'seen' as being related.

Neisser offered a combined view, suggesting that perception is sometimes bottom-up and sometimes top-down. For example, colour perception is largely innate and physically-based whereas some aspects of depth perception (such as texture gradients or linear perspective) are learned and explained by top-down processes.

| **Examiner's tip** | The third part of this answer is again coherent and well-detailed in terms of what is there. However, it is somewhat repetitive and perhaps closer to 'limited' rather than 'appropriate'. On balance though, it probably belongs in the top band. An examiner might (unofficially) think in terms of a rule of thumb when marking it: if the candidate only mentioned one kind of perceptual process or one opposing theory, the answer would be placed in the bottom band, however if there is a good degree of elaboration the answer might move into the next band. For the top band, the examiner is looking for more processes and/or theories, elaboration and empirical support. |

Question 2

| **Examiner's tip** | This is a good example of the kind of question which is easily misread. An anxious exam candidate sees the words 'selective attention' and rushes into their standard essay on the theories of attention. But wait, the question directs you to discuss 'experimental studies'. Theoretical material will be relevant only if it is used to evaluate experimental work. So you might describe a particular study (Skill A) and evaluate it (Skill B) in terms of its theoretical value as well as the methodology. A candidate who makes no mention of theories could still achieve maximum marks if the experimental work is well evaluated. However, an answer which is all theory would receive no marks. |

Outline answer

1 Evidence related to single channel filter models:
- Broadbent (1958) dichotic listening task showed that processing was single channel.
- Support from Cherry (1953) cocktail party effect: subjects attend to physical aspects of non-attended message but meaning is lost.
- Theoretical interpretation: Broadbent's single channel filter model, messages filtered on basis of physical characteristics.
- Evaluation: experimental work shows that there is some processing after the initial filter.

2 Evidence that some processing occurs after the filter:
- Gray and Wedderburn (1960): subjects recall certain messages ('dear, 5, Jane' and '3, aunt, 4') by meaning.
- Treisman (1964): bilingual subjects given French and English messages presented separately to each ear with time delay. When delay decreased they realized the messages were the same.
- von Wright *et al.* (1975) paired certain words with electric shocks. When conditioned words presented to non-attended ear a GSR is produced.
- Theoretical interpretation: Treisman's attenuation model, filter just 'turns down' the non-attended sensory input. Some weak signals may trigger recognition.
- Evaluation: it is possible that experimental evidence can be explained by subjects rapidly switching from ear to ear.

3 Evidence for parallel processing:
- McKay (1973): subjects given sentence to non-attended ear which influenced their interpretation of an ambiguous word played to the attended ear. Suggests that unattended message is not just turned down because meaning is also processed.

- Theoretical interpretation: Deutsch and Deutsch's late selection model, parallel processing so there is no bottleneck.
- Evidence against: Treisman and Riley (1969) showed differences in detection rates between shadowed and non-shadowed ear.
- Alternative 'flexible' model: Johnston and Heinz (1978) showed extent of bottleneck depends on prevailing circumstances.
- Evaluation: models of central capacity (Kahneman) may ultimately offer a more comprehensive account.

4   Evaluation of experimental work:
  - It is laboratory-based and therefore lacks generalizability.
  - Laboratory subjects may experience experimenter bias so that their performance is not valid.
  - There are important practical applications, e.g. airline pilots.

Examiner's tip For a good answer the examiner would look for breadth in terms of the number of studies covered (at least 5 or 6 of them), depth in terms of the detail provided, and evaluation in terms of the study's theoretical value. The very best essays will include methodological criticisms as well, and would attempt to provide more than a 'list' of empirical studies. Note that evaluation can be in terms of applications as well.
Where only one study is discussed, the maximum mark would be 8.

Question 3

Examiner's tip This question is a gift to candidates who have prepared the topic of memory, because almost any material is relevant as long as its inclusion is justified. However, in general, only the most able candidates are able to offer such justification and also evaluate the material they present (Skill B).

Answer plan

1   Define 'types' to include process, storage system and memory trace.

2   Multistore approach and evidence: duration (Sperling, Peterson and Peterson), capacity (Miller), coding (Baddeley), brain damage (HM).

3   Subdivisions of LTM: Cohen and Squires, Tulving.

4   Levels of processing (an alternative approach is to explain memory in terms of processes instead of kinds of store).

5   Storage system itself: Collins and Quillan, McClelland.

6   Memory trace: iconic store.

Examiner's tip If you write an essay plan, do not cross it out. It may be helpful for the examiner to read it and note that you have a coherent strategy from the outset.

The word 'memory' actually refers to several things. It is the mental function of retaining data (i.e. learning), it is the storage system which holds the data and it is the data that is retained. Therefore, when discussing 'types' of memory we are justified in looking at different models or explanations of each of these.

The best known explanation of how data enters our memories is <u>Atkinson</u> and <u>Shiffrin's multistore model</u>. They suggested that information first appears in <u>sensory memory</u> (SM). It is then transferred to <u>short term memory</u> (STM) and, if it is rehearsed, it is placed in <u>long term memory</u> (LTM). There is a considerable body of empirical support for this view of qualitatively different kinds of storage.

<u>Sperling</u> (1960) conducted an experiment which provided evidence of a sensory store. Subjects were shown a grid of numbers or letters for less than one second. On some trials they were asked to recall everything and on other trials they were given a signal immediately after the display to indicate which row to report. Their recall was much better on the partial report condition which supported the view that the information held in SM decays rapidly if not accessed immediately.

<u>Peterson and Peterson</u> (1959) presented trigrams and asked subjects to recall them after a time delay. If the delay was 3 seconds, the subjects' recall was around 80%. If the delay was 18 seconds, recall fell to 10%. This supports the idea that STM is different from LTM in terms of duration.

There is evidence to show that STM has a limited capacity whereas LTM is potentially unlimited. <u>Miller</u> (1956) reviewed research into STM and concluded that the span of STM is about 7 ± 2 bits of information. He said you can increase this capacity if you chunk bits of information into meaningful units. This research has useful applications, for example in the design of post codes and telephone numbers.

Another difference between STM and LTM lies in the way information is coded. <u>Baddeley</u> (1966) gave subjects lists of words which were either acoustically or semantically similar. When they were then asked to recall immediately (STM) they showed acoustic confusion, whereas if recall was after one minute (LTM) they showed semantic confusion.

A different kind of evidence comes from studies of brain damage. One such study was of <u>H.M.</u>, a severe epileptic who had his hippocampus removed to help his seizures. His LTM remained intact but he was unable to store any new information (STM). This evidence has the disadvantage that it is a case study and therefore any generalizations should be treated cautiously. The fact that he had brain damage also means that the evidence may not represent normal behaviour.

Several psychologists have offered refinements of the multistore model. <u>Cohen and Squire</u> (1980) divided LTM into a <u>procedural system</u> and a <u>declarative system</u>. These are knowledge about how to do things and knowledge about facts, respectively. <u>Tulving</u> (1972) further divided declarative memory into <u>episodic memory</u>, which is memory for personal events and people, and <u>semantic memory</u>, which is memory about language and general knowledge. These distinctions are important because they explain the behaviour of amnesiacs. Such people do not lose all their

memory, their procedural system generally remains intact. These distinctions are also important because they highlight a problem with memory research generally. It is usually laboratory based and concentrates on episodic memory. For this reason such experiments lack everyday validity.

> **Examiner's tip** The last two paragraphs contain useful evaluations, contributing to the quality of the essay.

An alternative approach is to explain memory in terms of processes instead of kinds of store. This is the levels of processing model first suggested by Craik and Lockhart (1972). They argued that what mattered was how deeply information is processed rather than rehearsal. 'Depth' is measured in terms of meaning; the more meaningful a piece of data the more likely it will be remembered. Rehearsal is one means of making information meaningful, but it is not the only way. Craik and Tulving (1975) demonstrated this in an experiment where subjects were shown a list of words and after each word they had to answer a question. There were different kinds of question which either led to shallow, phonemic or semantic processing. For example, the subject was asked to write down a word that rhymed with the stimulus word (phonemic processing) or to write a sentence for the word (semantic). Semantic processing led to greatest recall. In this experiment no one was asked to memorize or learn anything, memory occurred naturally as a result of undertaking semantic processing. Mandler (1967) did a similar thing in an experiment where subjects had to sort packs of cards with words on them. At the end they were able to remember the words they had sorted even though they had not been asked to do so. They had memorized them during the task of organizing them.

All of these are models suggest how data is retained. Other models describe the storage system itself. For example, Collins and Quillan (1969) suggested that items are stored in LTM in a hierarchical network. Empirical support for this comes from a study by Bower et al. (1969) who gave subjects words either jumbled up or in categories. When the words were arranged in conceptual hierarchies, recall was considerably better. An alternative model is drawn from computer technology, for instance McClelland (1981) described memory as a connectionist network where parallel distributed processing occurs. Each individual memory is stored in several interconnected units rather than a single place and therefore recall involves accessing a number of nodes.

Finally, there are different types of memory in terms of the way memory is stored. Some memories may be stored linguistically whereas others are visual. For example, Tolman found evidence for cognitive maps. Shepard and Metzler (1971) demonstrated visual representation in an experiment where they showed subjects a visual image and then the same image rotated. The greater the rotation the longer it took for subjects to identify whether the object was the same as the original stimulus. This means that they must have some visual representation which they were rotating in their mind.

The evidence presented here shows that there are many different types of memory and suggests that advice about memory needs to be different for different kinds of memory.

Answers to Unit 5

Question 4

There is much evidence to support the view that language influences thought though there is also evidence for the position that it has no effect or that thought determines language.

An early behaviourist, Watson, suggested that language was thought. He said that thinking occurs in the voice box. However, Smith demonstrated that he could think even when his voice box was paralysed using a drug. The drug paralysed all his muscles and when it wore off he was able to report his thoughts and perceptions. Furth studied deaf children and showed that they had near normal intelligence, therefore supporting Smith's criticisms.

Whorf and Sapir produced a theory referred to as the Sapir–Whorf Hypothesis. At its strongest this theory states that language _determines_ thought. Whorf said that language 'cuts nature up'. He thought that if you did not have a particular word in your vocabulary it would be very difficult to have the concept. Carroll and Casangrande provided evidence to support this view. They compared Navaho and American children and found that Navaho children were better at form recognition. They supposed that this was because their language stressed the importance of form. It is possible that the researchers did not fully understand the Navaho children (a problem with cross-cultural research) and the differences may be due to experience rather than language.

Whorf later suggested that linguistic determinism may be too strong a concept and that linguistic _relativity_ is more accurate; this is called the Linguistic Relativity Hypothesis. This states that language _influences_ the way you think. The classic example given for this is that the Eskimos have many different words for snow and this makes it possible for them to make distinctions between types of snow which

English speakers cannot. Pinker calls this the 'Great Eskimo Vocabulary Hoax' because he says that English speakers actually have access to as many words for snow as the Eskimos (e.g. slush, powder, avalanche). He says that it is the need to make distinctions which leads people to invent vocabularies or to use existing terms. For example, if you breed horses you come to learn many different words for size, shapes, colours, gender and ages of horses. This suggests that cognitive need drives language rather than *vice versa*.

However, Loftus *et al.* (1978) showed that language can alter perception. When they asked subjects to recall some pictures their answers were different depending on whether they said 'Did you see the broken headlight?' or 'a broken headlight'. This is because the word 'the' suggests that there was a headlight whereas 'a' means there may or may not have been one. Carmichael *et al.* (1932) showed that language can alter memory. They showed subjects a set of ambiguous pictures, each described with a label. For example, a picture of two circles joined by a line was described either as a dumbbell or a pair of glasses. When the subjects were later asked to draw the pictures they had seen, their drawings were influenced by the label they had been given.

drawing by someone told it is a dumbell

drawing by someone told it is a pair of glasses

Just because language sometimes does affect our perception or memory this does not mean that it <u>always</u> does. Rosch (1978) taught some natives from New Guinea some colour words. This particular tribe only had two colour words in their language and these were for black and white. Rosch found that they were quicker at learning a new colour category based on fire-engine red than a category based on off-red. She suggested that this is because fire-engine red is the colour that the cones in our eye respond best to. In this case language did not influence their perception, instead perception affected their language. Again this is cross-cultural research so we should be cautious about the evidence.

Various developmental psychologists have also expressed views on the relationship between language and thought. Vygotsky said that language and thought start independently, a baby thinks without words (pre-verbal thought) and babbles without meaning (pre-intellectual speech). When they start to use words these words shape the way they think. But Vygotsky did suggest that learning a word is the <u>beginning</u> of learning a new concept and not the end.

Piaget suggested that, if anything, thought could be said to determine language rather than *vice versa*. In Piaget's view cognitive development is not helped by language; children only learn words after they have learned the concepts. There is some evidence to support his views. Sinclair-de-Zwart found linguistic differences between children who could and could not conserve. The ones who could conserve were able to use comparative terms such as 'bigger' whereas the nonconservers had more limited vocabularies, for example, they used 'small' to mean short, thin, and few. She tried to teach these verbal skills to the nonconservers but they were still unable to conserve. Therefore just being given an appropriate vocabulary does not seem to lead to cognitive advances.

As we can see there are occasions when language does influence thought and when thought influences language. There are also occasions when they are independent.

6   DEVELOPMENTAL PSYCHOLOGY

Question 1

'Mother love in infancy and childhood is as important for mental health as are vitamins and proteins for physical health' (Bowlby, 1951).

Prior to Bowlby, the dominant psychological view from both the Behaviourists and Freudians was that the caregiver's primary concern was to provide food and physical comfort. In the 1950s Bowlby challenged this view with the argument given in the quotation. He said that mother love (emotional care) was equally important and that deprivation of such love had consequences as severe as malnutrition. This is called the maternal deprivation hypothesis. Bowlby also proposed the concept of monotropy, that is the need for one central caregiver, usually the mother but it could be the father or another person. Bowlby also felt that there was a critical period in the formation of attachment bonds. He believed that children who experience maternal deprivation under the age of 4 will suffer permanent damage.

Bowlby's views were supported by three important pieces of empirical evidence. First there was his own research called 'Forty-four juvenile thieves' (1946). Bowlby looked at the life histories of 88 children who had been referred to his psychiatric clinic, half of whom had a criminal record for theft. Fourteen of the 'thieves' displayed an 'affectionless' character. Almost all of these affectionless children had been separated from their mothers before they were 2, whereas this was not true for the other 'thieves'. This is good evidence but it should be regarded cautiously because it was collected retrospectively and people do not always remember past events accurately. It is also correlational and therefore we cannot be sure whether the separations themselves caused the maladjustment or whether, for example, general family discord was a cause.

A second piece of important empirical support came from Lorenz (1935). He demonstrated that goslings will become attached to the first figure they see upon hatching. In birds this process is called imprinting and only occurs during a critical period; a few days after hatching the goslings would not have imprinted on Lorenz. Bowlby suggested that attachment behaviour is a kind of imprinting, that human infants are born with an innate tendency to form a close bond with their caregiver and this will ensure food and safety, in the same way that imprinting is important for birds. Klaus and Kennell (1976) found that infants who are separated from their mothers during the first 12 hours after birth may suffer long-term consequences in terms of poor attachment. However, subsequent research has not consistently supported this finding.

The third piece of evidence came from Harlow's work with rhesus monkeys (1959). He provided an infant monkey with two 'mothers', one a wire cylinder with a monkey-like face and a feeding bottle attached, the other with no feeding bottle but wrapped in a cloth. Behaviourists and Freudians would predict that the monkeys should become attached to the 'mother' that offered food rather than comfort. In fact, the monkeys spent most of their time with the cloth mother, visiting the other one only for food. When they were frightened they always went to the cloth mother. In later life the monkeys raised without a responsive mother were socially maladjusted and had difficulty with mating and parenting. This supports Bowlby's views in several ways. First it shows that the monkeys primarily sought emotional care, poor as it was, and second that this poor substitute for maternal care had important consequences for later psychological development.

Harlow's research was very influential but has been criticized for the lack of concern shown to the experimental subjects. The results should also be treated with caution because we are generalizing from animal to human behaviour which is not always appropriate. The same criticism applies to Lorenz's evidence.

Examiner's tip The candidate has presented comments on methodology after each study. This is a good habit because it ensures that you are providing Skill B material.

Not all psychologists agreed with Bowlby's views. Some of his claims were challenged by Schaffer and Emerson (1964). They followed 60 newborn babies over a period of 18 months and found that the infants formed multiple attachments rather than just one. In fact many societies rely on multiple attachments, for example, Ainsworth (1967) found this is true for the Ganda tribe of Uganda.

Schaffer and Emerson also found that it was the quality rather than the quantity of care which was important. Ainsworth called this the 'caregiving hypothesis' – secure attachment occurs when a mother is sensitive, sees things from the infant's viewpoint, and is accepting. Bowlby's theory suggested that the amount of time spent with the infant was crucial for good attachment and that mothers should not go out to work or their children would suffer emotional deprivation. Research on kibbutzim in Israel by Fox (1977) showed that children remained most attached to their mothers despite the fact that they spent more time with a metapelet in the Children's House. It may be that the children were not as attached to their metapelets because there was quite a high turnover. However, the research does show that there are many different ways to raise children. Research which looks at the effects of day care, such as Kagan et al. (1980), has also found that children suffer no emotional and cognitive deprivation due to maternal separation. In fact in some cases children may benefit.

A more critical issue was raised by Rutter (1981) who felt that the main problem with the concept of maternal deprivation was that it muddled together a range of essentially different experiences. Rutter felt that separation is not the crucial factor in emotional disturbance and that general family discord may be more critical. Rutter also felt that deprivation should be distinguished from privation. Deprivation is the disruption of a bond whereas privation is the failure to form any bonds in the first place. Bowlby's thieves may be examples of privation, as is the case for institutionalized children. Tizard and Hodges (1978) study of institutionalized children found that those who were adopted before the age of 4 showed good recovery whereas those who returned home fared even worse than those who remained in care. Therefore maternal deprivation may be something children can recover from. The study again shows that it is the quality of the bonds which is important.

It is also true that short separations may in themselves cause distress to children rather than the bond disruption itself. A hospital stay may be a frightening experience for a young child. The Robertsons found that children who were separated from their parents for short periods remained emotionally stable if they were offered substitute mothering, in addition to physical care.

In conclusion, we should return to the original quotation which suggests that mother love is vital for healthy development. The evidence shows that it is, but that it can be received from many sources not just the mother, and it is the quality not the quantity that is important in healthy attachment. This does not mean that Bowlby was wrong but that some of his views need modifying.

Examiner's tip The essay provides a good balance between supporting and criticizing Bowlby's views. It starts with a sound description of his theory and then uses empirical evidence to critically evaluate the validity of his claims both positively and negatively. The material has been well selected and presented critically and coherently. Some of the evidence which is commonly used by candidates (e.g. Freud and Dann, studies of isolated children) is well omitted because it is out of date and based on unusual and limited samples. However, many candidates do use this evidence and it gains marks where appropriate. Try to include the best available evidence.

An essay which focused on only two or three pieces of empirical evidence would probably be placed at the top of band 1, gaining around 7 or 8 marks.

Question 2

Examiner's tip The question specifies that you select only one theory; writing about more than one leaves the examiner with the choice of which to mark but is not a good exam strategy because it wastes time and will rarely receive much more than half marks.

Piaget's theory will be the most obvious one to select because it is covered comprehensively in textbooks and its applications to education are well documented. Vygotsky is becoming a viable alternative. Whatever theory you choose must be used in both parts of the question, though in part (b) you could use one theoretical approach as a means of critically evaluating the other.

Behaviourist theory is not really a theory of cognitive development because behaviourists do not acknowledge mental states, however it could be used if a case for it is argued (e.g. that it accounts for learning and intelligent behaviour).

Part (a) is description only and therefore any evaluation you include here would attract no marks. Part (b) is tied to part (a); for good marks you must indicate that you are applying the theory in part (a) to education. It should not just be a general discussion of applying theories of cognitive development to education.

The question says 'application<u>s</u>' and therefore you must cover two or more. You could aim for breadth and mention lots, each with some supporting psychological material, or take the 'depth route' and cover only two or three but each with empirical support.

(a) Piaget's theory of cognitive development has been called one of genetic epistemology. This is because it presents a view of the child's developing intellect based on biological and innate processes. There are two strands to his theory: the structure of the intellect and the stages through which development proceeds.

<u>The structure of the intellect</u>   There are innate cognitive structures which enable us to assimilate and accommodate knowledge. An infant is born with certain innate schema, such as sucking or grasping schema. These are accommodated or modified when the infant experiences new information which does not fit the existing schema. The driving force in this process is a desire for equilibrium. When the existing schema does not match present experience a state of disequilibrium occurs and the infant must reorganize its schema to fit the new information. If new information fits with the existing schema the process of assimilation takes place whereby the new information is understood within the existing structure. Assimilation and accommodation are invariant processes because they remain the same throughout life, whereas schema and operations are variant ones because they are constantly changing as a result of new experiences.

Operations are higher order mental structures which involve physical or symbolic manipulations. As children mature their brains are able to function at progressively more abstract and less egocentric levels. According to Piaget this development is not a result of experience but of maturation. No amount of teaching should enable a child to perform certain operations until s/he is ready.

<u>Stages of development</u>   The first is the sensorimotor stage (0–2 years), so-called because the infant is focused on mainly sensory and motor experiences. The first schema are innate, reflex activities, such as sucking. Next the infant displays primary and secondary circular reactions, such as kicking and smiling. These are called circular because they are repetitive. By the age of 8 months the infant starts to co-ordinate existing schema to deliberately solve problems such as lifting something up to see what is underneath. The infant also develops a sense of object permanence – searching for an object when it has moved out of sight.

First words appear around the age of one. Piaget considered that language is an outcome of thought. This signals the end of the sensorimotor stage because the infant no longer relies on the physical representation of things. The actual ages that Piaget described are not fixed but the sequence of these stages is critical. Piaget also pointed out that development does not always proceed smoothly but instead that a child may be able to perform a particular operation in one context but not another because of different learning experiences. This is called horizontal décalage.

Examiner's tip   These two points are evidence of a high degree of understanding of Piaget's theory.

The second stage is called the pre-operational stage, and is divided into a pre-conceptual stage (2–4 years) and an intuitive stage (4–7). Children in this stage can form and use symbols, for example, in speaking and counting. Thought processes are developing but are still unsystematic (syncretic). Behaviours which are characteristic of this stage include: animism, egocentric thought, centration, moral realism, and the inability to perform concrete operations such as conservation and reversibility. Children of this age can do some reasoning but cannot use adult logic.

The third stage is the stage of concrete operations (7–11). This involves more adult-like thought but it is still not abstract, totally systematic nor always using adult logic. The child can now cope with conservation, centration, seriation, class inclusion, understanding numbers and reversibility.

Piaget said that from 11 years onwards thinking reached the stage of formal operations though there is some disagreement about whether all adults ever reach this stage. At this stage a person is capable of abstract and systematic deduction and induction.

Examiner's tip Notice here that specific examples have rarely been included; time does not permit such detail and what is provided here is amply sufficient for a top mark. A candidate who limits their description to Piaget's 'ages and stages' would receive no more than a band 2 mark and a bare outline would be a band 1.

(b) Piaget's theory had an enormous effect on classroom practice. His theory suggested that maturation and readiness are of critical importance in cognitive development and therefore outside influences should have a minimal effect. It is important to wait until a child is ready before they are taught new operations. The teacher may assess readiness through various class activities, such as doing work with rhyming sounds before teaching pupils to read.

Piaget also thought that self-discovery and self-motivation are critical in developing intrinsic satisfaction. This approach is called 'discovery learning'. Piaget recommended that the teacher's role is not to impart knowledge but to ask questions and thus motivate the child to discover things for themselves. The teacher may also create situations which lead a child to ask their own questions. Children may work in small groups and influence each other, again through questions. The importance of these questions lies in the fact that they create disequilibrium in the child's existing schema and force the child to make accommodations.

Examiner's tip This is a good example of using knowledge about Piaget's theory to make sense of his recommendations for educational practice.

This approach involves individualized learning rather than class teaching. It has had most influence in nursery and primary school but has also been important in the development of certain Maths and Science programmes for older children, such as the Nuffield Project which relies on children making their own discoveries and being involved in practical exercises.

Piaget's approach is different from Bruner or Vygotsky who both thought that cognitive development depends on the guidance of those with greater knowledge, not just in questioning the child but in directing them about what to do.

Examiner's tip The candidate is using knowledge of other theories to evaluate Piaget's approach.

Freund (1990) investigated the value of intervention with preschool children playing with a doll's house and who were then assessed on a furniture sorting task. Those who worked with their mothers showed dramatic improvement whereas another group who worked on their own changed very little. This supports Vygotsky's view that guidance increases learning, though it could be argued that the mothers were just questioning the children, as Piaget recommends, and thus encouraging cognitive development.

Another experiment by Bradley and Bryant (1983) showed that training preschool children in sound categorization skills led to significant improvements in reading. On the other hand Gibson *et al.* (1962) found that children under 5 had more difficulty with a letter recognition task than slightly older children. This suggests that maturational factors may be involved.

Ausubel suggested that discovery learning is time-consuming and often impossible in secondary education, whereas reception learning is more efficient. For example, Ausubel suggested the use of 'advanced organizers' which enable a student to be presented with a framework for organizing new material, a bit like being given the outline of a lecture.

The same issues can be applied to education outside the classroom. Parents, playleaders and toy manufacturers are interested in knowing what to do for the best. Piaget's theory would suggest that children need activities appropriate for their maturational stage and they should be left largely to their own investigations. Vygotsky's view would be that adults should show children what to do.

Examiner's tip Part (b) acts as a good discriminator because some candidates will not be able to write anything, whereas others will be able to present a reasonable argument about education based on their theory of cognitive development. It is helpful to include contrasting theories by way of evaluation and/or also to use empirical evidence to support your arguments.

Question 3

Examiner's tip The question requires you to describe and evaluate both psychodynamic and social learning theories of moral development. Cognitive-developmental theories will only be relevant in so far as they are used to evaluate the other approaches.
When describing psychodynamic theory you should take care to include only material which is relevant; details of Freud's general theory of development will receive little credit. Where possible your description should be supported by empirical evidence (Skill B) and you should include details of the advantages and disadvantages of each approach.

This essay will describe and evaluate psychodynamic (Freudian) and social learning theories of moral development. At the end some comparisons will be made with the third major approach to moral development, the cognitive-developmental one.

Examiner's tip This is a useful introductory paragraph because it helps both you and the examiner to have an organized picture of what is to come.

Freud believed that moral behaviour is controlled by the superego, which develops during the phallic stage, around the age of 3. At this time the child's interest focuses on their genitalia and they feel desire for their opposite-sex parent. This makes them see their same-sex parent as a rival. The child feels unconscious hostility, resulting in guilt. The child also feels anxiety and fear of punishment should his true desires be discovered. Resolution occurs through identification with the same-sex parent. Identification is the process of 'taking on' the attitudes and ideas of another person. This identification results in the formation of the conscience and ego-ideal, which embody the moral values of the same-sex parent.

Identification is also important for gender identity and attitudes towards authority. Unsatisfactory resolution results in problems such as amorality, homosexuality or rebelliousness.

Freud referred to this as the Oedipus complex in boys because Oedipus was a figure in Greek mythology who loved his mother and killed his father. In girls, the same process is termed the Electra complex. The young girl has 'penis envy' and resents her mother for not providing her with one. A girl does not resolve this through identification, therefore according to Freud, girls do not reach moral maturity.

Your ego-ideal rewards you when you behave in accordance with parental moral values, acting as the 'rewarding' parent. Your conscience, which develops around the age of 5, acts as the 'punishing' parent and creates a sense of guilt. Freud predicted an inverse relationship between guilt and discipline because a child raised leniently will identify more with their parents and should therefore have a stronger conscience and a greater sense of guilt. Children who do not identify with their parents should have a weaker conscience.

There are both advantages and disadvantages to Freud's account of moral development. In general Freud made a great contribution to psychology by emphasizing the importance of early childhood. Other theories and research agree with Freud's view of developing gender awareness and a sense of conscience between the ages of 3 and 5.

On the other hand, there is little empirical evidence to support his theories and his theory is rather limited in that it does not explain female development nor does it explain how children from one parent families manage to develop a sense of morals and gender identity. Freud's view assumes that morals are unconscious whereas people often think very carefully about what they are going to do, for example, a decision to become a vegetarian. The notion of a conscience suggests that people will behave consistently whereas there is evidence that they do not (Hartshorne and May, 1928).

Freud's theory and the social learning theory both use the concepts of reward and punishment and identification. Social Learning Theory (SLT) suggests that children learn what is right and wrong either through direct reinforcement, or indirectly, by seeing what others do and whether or not they are rewarded or punished. Children imitate people they identify with. Bandura's research (1961) with Bobo the doll was a demonstration of how children learn new behaviour through vicarious reinforcement.

The main source of learning comes from parents. Hoffman (1970) found that moral development could be related to style of discipline but that punishment was not the most effective method. Parents who use a style of discipline called 'power assertion' may create a sense of anger or resentment whereas the 'inductive' method leads to more mature moral development. This method involves the parent explaining why a behaviour is wrong and emphasizing how it affects others. However, this research was correlational, which means that you cannot say for sure that parental style caused more mature moral development. It could be that the child's level of moral development dictates the kind of punishment their parents use. For example, children who are morally less well-developed need more coercive forms of punishment whereas children who are already morally sophisticated can be reasoned with.

Rewards may also be counterproductive as Lepper et al. (1973) showed in a field experiment with preschool children. Those children who were told that they would receive a reward for drawing a picture performed less well than those children who were not prewarned. This empirical evidence suggests that both parents and teachers should not rely on punishments and rewards as a means of teaching

children right and wrong. Hartshorne and May also found in their study of moral behaviour that efforts to teach children directly about right and wrong were less successful than indirect methods.

Rosenhan (1970) looked at why some people behave more prosocially than others. He interviewed people who had been involved in the 1960s US civil rights movement and found that those who were fully committed had warmer relations with their generally liberal parents and their parents were people who did prosocial things rather than just talking about it. Their parents acted as prosocial models rather than instructors and, because they had warmer relations, the children identified more with their parents.

Bryan and Test (1967) showed that people do behave more prosocially if they see other people doing it. People who drove past a broken down car were more likely to stop if they had seen someone else helping a motorist earlier on.

SLT can explain moral inconsistency because children learn that certain behaviours are not acceptable in some situations whereas they are in others. Another advantage of the SLT approach is that it has stimulated a lot of research because it makes clear predictions and some research provides good empirical support, unlike psychodynamic theory.

Some negative points have already been mentioned, such as the counterproductive nature of solely using reward and punishment. SLT also excludes the possibility of conscious decisions rather than conditioned responses. SLT does not account for the fact that children seem to pass through different stages of moral behaviour, which is something that cognitive-developmental theory does. Piaget and Kohlberg both have evidence that children's moral behaviour changes as they get older. For example, Piaget found that younger children are heteronomous – their morals are taken from others and they are more concerned with consequences rather than intentions. Children aged over 9 are autonomous – they have begun to work out their own sense of right and wrong and this takes intentions into account. This view suggests that moral development is related to cognitive maturation processes.

Examiner's tip Some students may find it difficult to resist including the wealth of material they have revised about Piaget and Kohlberg – but do resist. Almost all of it will be uncreditworthy and, though the examiner will not deduct marks for irrelevant material, you will be wasting time which could have been better spent organizing a coherent essay including what you do know about the theories in question.

The answer given here demonstrates top band skills such as coherence, selectivity (with regard to Freud's theory and the cognitive-developmental material), good use of evidence, well detailed descriptions and a good understanding of the two theories. The answer is balanced, giving material relevant to both theories. Candidates who describe only one approach would receive a maximum of 16 marks.

Question 4

Examiner's tip You must base the essay on some identifiable theory and not just a collection of empirical findings. This could be a recognized theory of adulthood (e.g. Erikson's or critical life event theory), or you could use more universal approaches (e.g. social learning theory) or concentrate on one aspect of adult behaviour (e.g. intelligence).

You should describe one theory only, though other approaches can be used in evaluation.

Outline answer

1 Introduction/background for Erikson's theory of lifespan development: Erikson is a neo-Freudian. Called 'ego psychology' since he de-emphasized the unconscious and emphasized the social world. He wrote about psychosocial rather than psychosexual (Freudian) stages.

2 The theory:

- There are 'eight stages of man' which cover the whole lifespan. Each stage of life is marked by a crisis, which must be confronted and resolved. The stages are universal.

- Stages 1–5 are concerned with the period from birth to the age of 18. Stage 5 is called 'adolescence' and is resolved by developing a coherent personality and finding a vocation. An individual who fails to resolve this crisis becomes a confused adult.

- Stage 6 is young adulthood (age 20–40), intimacy versus isolation. The main task is to develop lasting relationships. Failure results in isolation. Friends and lovers help.

- Stage 7 is middle adulthood (age 40–64), generativity versus stagnation. The main task is to be productive for society. Failure results in a sense of boredom and self-involvement. Your spouse and children are most important.

- Stage 8 is late adulthood (age 65+), integrity versus despair. The main task is to review and evaluate life, leading to either a sense of satisfaction and acceptance of death, or regrets and fear of death. Important people are your spouse, children, grandchildren.

3 Empirical support:

- Case studies of Indians and Second World War veterans indicated how ego development is related to social influences. These studies led Erikson to propose an alternative to psychosexual development.

- Psychohistories: studied biographies of famous people such as Freud and Luther.

4 Positive points:

- Suggests that development continues throughout life rather than the Freudian view that childhood is critically important.

- Incorporates social as well as biological influences.

- Provides a useful framework for co-ordinating other views, e.g. critical life events.

5 Negative points:

- Rather vague about the causes of social development.

- Rather loose collection of ideas; is it a theory?

- Lacks empirical support, based on own observations.

- Somewhat outdated because some people retire later or become parents later. It may be more appropriate to think in terms of common events rather than things common to certain ages, i.e. critical life event theory.

6 Alternative theories for particular ages of adulthood:

- Young adulthood: Coleman's Focal Theory.

- Middle adulthood: marriage, divorce, parenting, employment (critical life events).

- Late adulthood: disengagement or activity theory.
- Lifespan theories: Levinson's seasons of adulthood and/or Gould's transitions. These offer a more fluid approach.

7 Conclusion: the enduring use of Erikson's stages suggest that it expresses some important elements of lifespan development.

Examiner's tip Erikson is perhaps the best choice because of the availability of information. Alternatives include: Freud (though care needs to be taken to focus on adulthood rather than childhood), Piaget (again difficult), Kohlberg (slightly easier) or critical life events which count as a theory (see AEB glossary of terms in the Introduction).

7 PERSPECTIVES IN PSYCHOLOGY

Question 1

Examiner's tip The instruction to 'critically consider' means that you should demonstrate knowledge and understanding of the issue (Skill A) and show an awareness of the strengths and limitations of the arguments presented (Skill B). Skill B marks are also awarded for the breadth of your discussion, drawing on different areas of the syllabus.

The question is whether people are free to choose what they do (free will) or whether their behaviour is predetermined by other forces (a determinist view).

The philosophers Locke, Berkeley and Hume all thought that human behaviour is the result of forces over which we have no control. There are many psychological approaches which take a determinist stand; some explain behaviour in terms of external or environmental factors and others use internal factors.

The behaviourists would say that our behaviour is determined by external factors. We may think that we are exercising free will but in fact all our behaviour has been conditioned from an early age. We start life as a tabula rasa (blank slate) and our behaviour is progressively shaped through positive and negative reinforcement, punishment and rewards. Skinner's theory of language acquisition is an example of this. He claimed that children learn language because they are rewarded when a noise they make results in someone doing something, such as their mother giving them some milk. Infants start by making random noises called mands and through shaping these come to sound more and more like the real word.

Examiner's tip This is a good example of using knowledge gained in other areas of the syllabus to support your arguments. The evidence cited is reasonably well detailed. The candidate goes on to present some evaluation of Skinner and behaviourism.

Other psychologists such as Chomsky say that language acquisition is a result of innate capabilities not just conditioning. The main criticism of the behaviourist approach is that it may explain animal behaviour but human behaviour is more complex and not just a question of stimulus and response. It is also reductionist, oversimplifying more complex processes. Nevertheless it does explain certain aspects of behaviour and has had useful applications, such as in the treatment of psychological disorders.

Chomsky's views are an example of another kind of determinism – genetic determinism. This is the case when internal, genetic factors determine behaviour. Ethologists argue that we are born with innate characteristics which lead to specific behaviours. For example, Lorenz claimed that aggressive behaviour is the result of inherited predispositions which are triggered by environmental stimuli. In one experiment Lorenz (1951) showed that a male stickleback will attack anything which is red. Animal aggression rarely results in real harm (except in predation) but modern warfare in humans prevents them being aware of the nonverbal signals which should stop their aggression. Presumably these nonverbal signals are innate, and similar to animal signals which indicate submission. Such knowledge suggests ways that people can try to reduce human aggression and warfare.

Bowlby's view of attachment is another example of genetic determinism. He said that infants are born with a drive to attach themselves to one main carer. If this does not occur during a critical period the child will suffer permanent emotional consequences. This theory had a large impact on how parents and other carers look after their children.

The ethological view of genetic (biological) determinism has been criticized because, like behaviourism, it applies more to animals. Human behaviour is much more influenced by learning than animal behaviour is, so that innate factors may have some effect on human behaviour but this effect is moderated by learning. This is called soft determinism, the view that certain factors predispose a person to specific behaviours but do not mean that the person has to behave in that way.

The physiological approach in psychology is an example of biological determinism. This approach seeks to explain all behaviour in terms of physiological activity. This is also a reductionist approach because it reduces complex behaviour to a simple set of units: nervous impulses and biochemical substances such as hormones. An example of this sort of explanation is that an emotional experience is the result of the release of adrenalin. James argued that we have an emotional experience because of the physiological reaction (we are frightened because we run) rather than the common-sense view that our body produces a physiological reaction as a consequence of cognitive sensations (we run because we feel frightened).

Physiological explanations are important in psychology because behaviour is clearly caused at one level by nervous impulses and brain activity. However, these explanations do not account for everything; as the Gestalt psychologists said the sum is greater than the individual parts. Human behaviour is also influenced by environmental factors, as suggested by the behaviourists.

Freud's theory is another kind of biological determinism. He claimed that adult personality is determined by early childhood experiences and these are governed by innate impulses. During the first year of life the id is dominant. This is the innate, unconscious part of the infant's personality. If the id is not satisfied through oral pleasure the child will become permanently fixated on oral gratification, for example becoming a smoker later in life. Therefore this view suggests that people do not have free will but they are driven to do things by unconscious innate desires and unresolved conflicts.

Subsequent psychoanalysts modified Freud's views and suggested that social factors were also important in determining adult personality. These neo-Freudians also felt that a person's conscious mind was capable of free will, as opposed to the

Freudian idea of the unconscious mind. This is the view taken up by humanists such as Carl Rogers. Rogers' client-centred therapy emphasized the fact that each person is in control of their own lives and that psychological health is promoted by taking charge. This view of free will includes the idea that if you decide to let others control you that is still an example of free will. This means in practice that it is hard to distinguish between free choice and situations where a person is unwittingly controlled by others. They may just think they are free.

Satre, an existential philosopher, went so far as to say that we are 'condemned to be free', that freedom is a great burden because it means that we must each be totally responsible for our behaviour and that we also must respect others' views. Laing's view of schizophrenia is an existential one. He felt that insanity was a sane response to an insane world and it is the observer and not the patient who is disturbed by the abnormal behaviour.

Ultimately free will means that everyone can do what they want which is probably not desirable or likely to happen. People need other people and therefore they conform to social pressures, another kind of determinism or at least soft determinism. If you take a determinist view, this means that people can disclaim responsibility for their actions. Some violent criminals have argued that their aggression is inherited and therefore they should not be punished for what they did.

An important consequence of the debate is whether scientific principles can be applied to the study of behaviour. If behaviour is entirely the consequence of free will the answer is no. Scientific research is based on the idea that behaviour is the result of predictable and consistent causes and effects. If there is some way in which behaviour is lawful then at least soft determinism is a valid approach.

Examiner's tip | Excellent reference to the consequences of the debate.

There is no reason for free will and determinism to be mutually exclusive. Behaviour may partly be the result of free will in conjunction with internal and external factors which influence what we are most likely to do. In some situations people are more likely to behave according to conscious decisions whereas in others they act unconsciously or as a result of outside influences. For example, if you decide to truant from school this may because past experience of truanting has been positively reinforcing therefore making it more likely that you would do it again. On the other hand, you may feel afraid that you might be punished if you are caught. At the time of making the decision you are free to choose on the basis of all the influences upon you.

Examiner's tip | This is an excellent answer; it is comprehensive and draws on a wide range of sources. The points which are made are effectively supported by detailed examples and critical evaluation. The arguments are coherently elaborated rather than simply being stated and there is a reasonable balance of material relevant to both sides of the debate. The candidate ends by considering the consequences of both approaches and a way of resolving the seeming dichotomy.
A candidate who writes only about free will or determinism would be given a maximum of 16 marks.

Question 2

Examiner's tip The question asks you to outline two theories (Skill A) and then evaluate them (Skill B) in terms of their gender bias. Skill B can also be demonstrated through the use of empirical research and other criticisms. Clearly you should select theories with a considerable degree of gender bias. The interpretation of the word 'theory' can include more general approaches such as the medical approach as long as you explain in what way this is a theory.

Developmental psychology is the most obvious area to concentrate on because such theories are more likely to include gender influences, however you should remember that marks will be awarded for your ability to draw on material from across the syllabus.

The two theories I will discuss are Kohlberg's theory of moral development and Freud's theory of personality development.

Kohlberg (1966) offered an elaboration of Piaget's cognitive-developmental account of moral development. It is cognitive because it approaches moral behaviour from the point of view of moral reasoning rather than Freud's more unconscious approach. It is developmental because it describes moral behaviour as something which changes through the course of childhood.

Kohlberg described three levels of moral development; each is divided into two stages. The first level is called the pre-conventional level (age 6–13). In the first stage of this level the child displays heteronomous morals. This means that their morals are those learned from others. Children at this age do what they are told and do not question authority. They are egocentric and do good to serve their own interests rather than because it is good for someone else.

The conventional level (age 13–16) is when children learn the conventions of their society. They continue to be unquestioning of authority and they conform to social mores.

The final level, the post-conventional or principled level (age 16–20) is a time when adolescents question authority and develop their own sense of what is right and wrong and value individual rights. The very last stage, stage 6 is the stage of universal principles which may not be reached by everyone.

Kohlberg and Colby conducted research (Colby et al., 1983) where they followed 58 men over a period of 20 years. The subjects were given moral dilemmas based on 10 moral issues such as punishment and justice. Each dilemma involves a conflict between two or more moral principles. One example is of the man whose wife is dying and needs an expensive drug. The druggist refuses to sell the drug cheaply to the man so he steals it. Was this right or wrong? Kohlberg classed moral development according to the reasoning revealed by the subjects' answers.

Examiner's tip Note the good level of understanding shown in the description of Kohlberg's theory. The candidate has not gone into excessive detail because of time limitations and the appropriateness for this question.

Colby et al. found that children exhibit different kinds of thinking at different ages, confirming Kohlberg's stages. Many criticisms have been made of this research and of Kohlberg's theory. A problem with the research is that the subjects were all men. This means that people accuse Kohlberg of having an androcentric theory, one which assumes that women behave the same as men. Carol Gilligan (1982) criticized Kohlberg's view based on her own studies of moral reasoning. She found that men and women behave differently; men are more oriented towards responsibility whereas women tend to put people before principles and are interested in relationships, caring and conformity. This is called the 'ethic of care'. Gilligan's view has an alpha-bias because it suggests that there are in fact important differences between men and women.

Kohlberg suggested that women were morally inferior to men; he found that they often developed no further than stage 3 (level 2). But the fact that his scheme is based on male values means that inevitably women will not score as highly. If Gilligan devised a stage theory based on female morality, men might appear to be morally immature.

Another criticism of Kohlberg is that he claimed that morals were universal rather than learned which would mean that male/female moral differences are innate. Other psychological research has found that most gender differences are learned (for example, Smith and Lloyd, 1978) which would lead us to suppose that the same is true for gender-related moral differences. If this aspect of moral behaviour is learned then it is likely that much of moral behaviour and principles are learned rather than being innate.

Freud lived in a society which believed that men were superior. Freud did not believe any differently. His theories reflect this attitude as they assume that the male is the basic model for human behaviour and that female behaviour should be considered within the same framework.

His theory basically suggested that we are born with certain innate desires which motivate our behaviour. Early experience is critical in forming adult personality. The first two stages of development, the oral and anal stages, are not related to gender. At this time the infant seeks satisfaction through their oral and anal erogenous zones. If pleasure is not achieved there are permanent consequences in terms of fixations and repressed desires.

The third stage occurs around the age of 3. This is the phallic stage when a child's sexual interest focuses on their genitalia and their parents. Freud also said that females were morally inferior to males because during the phallic stage a girl has 'penis envy' and resents her mother for not providing her with one. The father now becomes the love-object but this conflict cannot be resolved in the same way as it is for boys because the girl has no reason to identify with her same-sex parent and this means she cannot fully develop a conscience. There is no empirical evidence to support this view, which is a criticism in general of Freud's theory. As we have seen, Gilligan points out that females are indeed different but not inferior.

Freud suggested that girls resolve their penis envy by transferring their desire for a penis to their desire for children. Karen Horney (1939) argued that penis envy is actually an understandable envy of the status that men usually have in a patriarchal society. Erikson suggested that men have womb envy because females can create life. This means that men have a drive to create things and achieve more in life to overcome their envy. This view illustrates a different kind of gender bias, this time favouring women.

Freud's views are not entirely against women, in fact some feminists have suggested that his theory can be used to support a feminist position. For example, Williams (1987) argues that Freud's theory explains why women are oppressed. A girl's innate biological drives are modified by social influences so that when a girl lives in a patriarchal society she will learn that she is inferior whereas if she lived in a different society she would learn different attitudes about her gender. Therefore Freud shows how cultural conditioning creates a women's inferior status rather than that being necessarily the case.

This unusual view of Freudian theory contributes to the quality of the essay because it provides some balance and is evidence of wider reading.

Another gender bias in Freud's work is the fact that most of his patients were women and his theories are based on his observations of them. This led to a biased view of mental illness where hysteria was one of the main forms of illness. Freud's theories suggest that men have fewer problems with mental illness.

The importance of gender bias is that it perpetuates views of female inferiority and male superiority particularly where it suggests that this is innate rather than learned. The reason why most theories are gender biased is because their data is based on biased samples and is drawn from Western patriarchal society. Feminist approaches to psychology are important in redressing the balance, offering female viewpoints and encouraging critical thinking which avoids cultural and gender stereotypes and assumptions.

Examiner's tip This answer includes two theories which are described accurately and in sufficient detail to demonstrate a clear understanding. Freud's theory is somewhat sketchy but this is presumably due to time constraints and is balanced by the variety of material offered in relation to this theory.

The whole essay is well structured and coherent with minimal omissions. There is effective evaluation of the gender biases. At the end there is some attempt to discuss related issues (i.e. the effects of such biases and the importance of critical awareness).

If one theory is discussed then there would be a maximum of 16 marks.

Question 3

Examiner's tip Essays on animal research often attract ill-informed answers, based on descriptions of only one or two animal studies. Many candidates mistakenly equate 'research' with 'experiments' and write solely about animal experiments. They would do well to at least consider cases where experiments involve no suffering, though animal rights may still be compromised. Marks are awarded for an informed discussion rather than personal and anecdotal perspectives on animal research.

You should focus on the issues raised in the quotation. These are: whether humans are unique, whether research with animals is morally acceptable, and whether such research would have any practical value. It would be acceptable to discuss any other issues as long as at least two of the issues in the quotation are discussed.

Skill A will be demonstrated through a knowledge and understanding of the issues. Skill B will be shown in an ability to assess the validity of such claims through the use of empirical evidence and/or rational argument, as well as the coherence and detail of the answer. You should draw on material from across the syllabus, which will give breadth to your answer.

Outline answer

1   Why are animals used?

   • Advantages: quicker reproduction, simpler to study, fewer ethical problems, in some situations the only alternative (e.g. Blakemore's visual deprivation work), less problems with experimenter bias and demand characteristics.

   • Disadvantages: animals cannot report what they are thinking, ethical considerations.

2   Can the results of animal research be generalized to humans?

- Yes. Some aspects of human and animal behaviour are the same, e.g. studying the function of the nerves. Behaviourists argue that human and animal behaviour are qualitatively the same, e.g. the rules of operant conditioning can be applied to language acquisition and treating mental illness.

- No. Simply because structures are the same does not mean that they perform the same function. Human behaviour is much more affected by learning, e.g. selecting a mate. Humanists argue that humans are qualitatively different, e.g. language and self-awareness.

3 Is animal research morally acceptable/ethical?

- What do we mean by ethical? Do the ends justify the means?

- Yes, it is ethical. Some animal research involves no suffering and no interference, e.g. naturalistic observation. In some cases it is only recognized with hindsight that the research would cause the animals any suffering, e.g. Harlow's research with monkeys.

- No, it is not ethical. Do we know what animals feel? Singer (1993) suggests that we should legislate to put primates on a par with humans in terms of legal rights. Animals cannot give informed consent.

4 Does animal research have any practical value?

- No, not if animal data cannot be generalized to humans.

- Yes. The results of animal research may be used to improve the lives of animals in the wild. It is the only way to test certain psychological theories without endangering the lives of humans, e.g. Dement's work depriving cats of sleep. Animal research provides comparisons which may give useful insights into human behaviour, e.g. ethological research.

> **Examiner's tip** It is important to note that only psychological research is in question, therefore reference to the use and ethics of animals in medical research will not receive any marks.
> Candidates who address only one issue would receive a maximum of 16 marks. If the answer is not in some way tied to the quotation there would be a maximum of 20 marks.

8 RESEARCH METHODS IN PSYCHOLOGY

Question 1

> **Examiner's tip** Questions on this sub-section, the nature of psychological enquiry, are going to be about the uses, advantages and limitations of different kinds of research. You might be asked to list these or to make comparisons between different methods. You may also be tested on ethical considerations in relation to different methods.
> Use the marks to guide you in the length of answer required. Make sure that you provide sufficient detail to demonstrate your understanding and that you fulfil the rubric, i.e. where the question asks for two items make sure you do include two points.

(a) For example: highly controlled, manipulation of an independent variable, demonstrates cause and effect relationship unambiguously (any one).

(b) For example: location, extent of control over independent variable, control over participants, ethics of the manipulation, nature of research interest (any two).

(c) Advantage – for example: large sample can be tested, gives access to information not available from direct observation (any one).

Limitation – for example: cannot draw conclusions about causal relationships, may have social desirability bias, interviewer bias, sampling bias, people do not know what they think (any one).

(d) For example: deception, invasion of privacy, distress, informed consent, right to withdraw, confidentiality, debriefing (any two which are related to the interview method).

Examiner's tip In part (d) it is important to ensure that any ethical considerations that you provide are relevant to the interview method.

Question 2

Examiner's tip Make sure that each point that is made is adequately explained to demonstrate your understanding.

(a) Describe a particular sampling technique, such as random, opportunity, volunteer or quota. For example:

The researcher might use a random sampling procedure which could be achieved by putting the names of all the children in one school in a hat and selecting the number of children required for the study.

(b) Justify one of the following:
Independent groups, for example: no order or practice effects.
Repeated measures, for example: controls for subject variables, more sensitive statistics.
Matched participants, for example: no order or practice effects, subject variables partly controlled.

(c) The reliability of the study refers to the extent to which the questionnaire is consistent or dependable. There are various ways to maximize this, such as making sure that the children understand all of the questions, providing standardized instructions and providing sufficient choice of answers so that the children can select something which represents what they think.

Examiner's tip A candidate will receive full marks for each part of this question as long as the answer is accurate and includes some detail. Where a response is brief and/or muddled only one mark would be awarded.

Question 3

Examiner's tip Take note of the marks available for each question and tailor your answer accordingly. Always make it clear that you understand the words you use by amplifying your answer and providing sufficient detail.

(a) There is no difference in the behaviour of the animals before and after the new programme in terms of how settled they are.

(b) The time sampling method means that observations are made at regular intervals such as once every 5 minutes.

(c) The observers could have used event sampling, which would mean that a list of particular behaviours is drawn up and a frequency count kept of their occurrence.

(d) If only one observer is involved their view may be biased about what counts as unsettled behaviour. The data will be more reliable and valid if it comes from more than one person. This also makes sure that nothing is missed.

Examiner's tip A candidate will receive full marks for each part of this question as long as the answer is accurate and includes some detail. Where a response is brief and/or muddled only one mark would be awarded.

Question 4

Examiner's tip It is best to err on the side of too much detail though you should not spend more than 45 minutes on the whole question.

(a) A one-tailed test is one where the hypothesis has predicted the direction of the results. For example, saying that boys will do better than girls on a test rather than saying that their test scores will be different (two-tailed).

(b) There is a positive correlation between the personality scores of parents and their offspring.

Examiner's tip For one mark you must at least mention the fact that you are looking at a correlation. For the full two marks you must refer to both the direction of the hypothesis (positive) and the two variables (personality scores of parents and their offspring). Some psychologists prefer to write hypotheses in the future tense and to include the word 'significant' but this is not compulsory.

(c) The scores are measured on the ordinal scale. It is ordinal because observations have been placed in an order but the progression does not reflect true mathematical differences.

(d) The Spearman test was used because (1) it is a measure of the relationship between two variables i.e. a correlation, (2) the scores are ordinal rather than interval or ratio and (3) the scores are not known to have similar variances. Therefore a non-parametric test of correlation has been selected.

Examiner's tip Any three reasons could be presented; other possibilities include: the scores are not drawn from a normal population, the data does not fulfil parametric requirements, or the relationship between the two variables may not be linear. It is not sufficient to say that the researcher is looking for a correlation; this needs to be amplified to gain a mark.

(e) Significance level is the probability of a set of results occurring if only chance factors are operating. The student might have chosen the 5% level because this is the conventional level for this kind of research (not life threatening) and represents a good trade between a type I error (<u>rejecting</u> an alternative hypothesis which is in fact true) and a type II error (<u>accepting</u> an alternative hypothesis which is in fact wrong).

Examiner's tip The marks for this question are split equally between the first part (what is meant by 'significance level') and the second part (why choose 5%). The key points regarding significance level are that it expresses a probability about whether chance factors were responsible for the result. In the second half of the answer, it is not sufficient to just refer to type I and II errors, you need to demonstrate some understanding as well.

(f) You should draw a scattergraph. This would involve having the parent's personality score on one axis and the offspring's on the other. For each pair a cross can be drawn to indicate the relationship between the co-variables (parent and offspring personality score).

(g) For the mother–daughter relationship the correlation coefficient (0.62) for N = 10 exceeds the critical value (0.56) at the 5% level and therefore the result is significant. The mother–son coefficient (0.38) for N = 8 does not exceed the critical value (0.64) and therefore is not significant. The father–daughter coefficient (0.27) for N = 10 does not exceed the critical value (0.56) and therefore is not significant, and the father–son coefficient (0.88) for N = 8 exceeds the critical value (0.83) at the 1% level and therefore is highly significant.

(h) The correlations are significant for the pairings between same sex parents and offspring and not for opposite sex pairs. This suggests that children are more likely to imitate their same-sex parent probably because they identify more with them. This is a social learning explanation.

Examiner's tip One mark is given for an explanation and the further two marks for elaboration and/or relationship with some theoretical account.

(i) (1) I would select one mother and her daughter and ask if they would be able to take part in a case study, explaining what it will involve and gaining their informed consent. Next I would interview each of them and use a questionnaire to assess aspects of their personality. A case study should be a rich source of data so I would find out as much information about the participants as I could. This might mean conducting several interviews and perhaps even following the pair over months or years to see if the daughter became more or less like her mother.

Examiner's tip A good answer will mention various aspects of case studies and provide some detail. Weaker answers would cover only one or two points.

(2) Two problems with case studies are that they are biased and therefore it is hard to generalize from them, and they are time consuming.

(3) The advantage of a case study is that it provides knowledge in depth which could not be gained from one test of the participants. Case studies are open ended and therefore the researcher might come upon unexpected information which could lead to new avenues for research. A case study would be a useful way of looking at special cases which are atypical, such as a single parent mother and her daughter or an older mother and her daughter. Case studies have more real life validity.

9 APPLIED AND CONTEMPORARY PSYCHOLOGY

Question 1

(a) Two parapsychological phenomena are extrasensory perception (ESP) and psychokinesis. ESP is when a person is able to perceive something such as the picture another person is looking at without using any of the five senses. Psychokinesis is when a person influences a physical event without direct intervention such as lifting a table off the floor without touching it.

(b) Dear Mrs. Sceptic,
I was surprised to hear that you do not believe in paranormal phenomena. You must be unaware of the strong evidence which does exist. Obviously there are many anecdotal accounts which are suspect, though the number of people who are convinced by seances, reports of ghost sightings, out-of-body experiences and so on suggests that there may well be some truth in these reports. The problem is investigating them scientifically. It may be that such phenomena are not susceptible to this kind of research and we need to discover other techniques to prove their validity. I had one friend who was extremely down-to-earth and vividly told me of a ghost which regularly visited her house and was seen by more than one person. It's hard to explain her experiences except in terms of a ghost.

In fact there are some very good examples of scientific research. In parapsychology, for example, telepathy has been investigated using the Ganzfeld technique, introduced by Honorton (1974). The receiver is placed in total isolation, with ping-pong ball halves taped over their eyes, white noise played through headphones, and so on. The sender is also isolated and shown a picture randomly selected from a choice of four, which he concentrates on. The receiver tries to identify the image he is receiving out of the four possibilities. Honorton (1985) analysed 28 studies using the Ganzfeld technique and found that 38% of the time subjects were able to identify the correct picture. A chance level would be 25%, and therefore the result is highly significant. Hyman (1985) criticized the Ganzfeld work saying the experimental procedures were not rigorous enough but Honorton *et al.* (1990) designed a fully automated project which still produced significant results.

There is other scientific proof. Rhine (1934) developed the use of Zener cards, a pack of 25 cards with five symbols. The experimenter looks at each card and the subject reports what they think the experimenter is seeing. Rhine produced significant results. Soal and Bateman (1954) worked with a man called Basil Shackleton who produced results way beyond the chance level. It may be better to carry out research with selected individuals, like Shackleton, who are known to have paranormal capabilities and then the results of such experiments might be even better.

An interesting feature of paranormal research is that people who believe in such phenomena consistently perform better in research than nonbelievers. This what Schmeidler and McConnell (1958) found. They called believers 'sheep' and nonbelievers 'goats'. Some people say that perhaps an experimenter or subject who is a sheep will influence the results. On the other hand it could be that goats have a negative influence on research and this is why there is only a limited amount of hard evidence. It also suggests that if you had a paranormal experience this would change the way you feel about such phenomena.

Yours, Mrs. Believer

> **Examiner's tip** A good answer should contain at least three points and at least two empirical studies. An answer which includes only one study or one point would receive a maximum of 3 marks.

(c) Dear Mrs. Believer,

I happened to read the letter you sent to my friend about why you believe in paranormal phenomena. As a psychologist I am aware of many of the counter-arguments and, when I told our mutual friend, she thought I should send them to you as well, though you probably are well aware of them.

First of all, most of the so-called research into paranormal phenomena is highly unscientific and purely a matter of belief. Those few studies which you mention have been soundly criticized. Soal's research received a great deal of attention and he was accused of falsifying his data. Rhine's results were impressive but other researchers failed to replicate his work. Rhine suggested this was due to negative experimenter effects because the other investigators did not believe in paranormal phenomena.

As you mention, Hyman was very critical of Honorton's work and claimed that there were procedural errors and problems with the statistical analysis. He said that the most successful studies were those with the most flaws. When he analysed the same 28 studies he found that less than half of them had significant results, which might suggest that some experimenters produced significant results whereas others did not ('sheep' and 'goats'?).

Weil (1974) investigated the claims made by Uri Keller about being able to bend spoons and other paranormal abilities. At first Weil was convinced until James Randi, a magician, demonstrated the same feats and showed Weil how they were done. Weil concluded that what we perceive is not the same as what is real, that our beliefs and perceptions alter what we perceive.

This, and the fact that 'sheep' produce positive results, suggests that paranormal phenomena can be explained in terms of an experimenter bias and self-fulfilling prophecy – the fact that a person's beliefs alter events and thus confirm their original expectations. In an experiment researchers may unknowingly communicate their expectations to their subjects and change their behaviour in the desired direction. A well known example of this was the horse 'Clever Hans' who appeared to be able to add, until people realized that the horse's trainer was subtly and maybe unconsciously giving cues about what the horse should do.

Believers collect evidence which supports their view and overlook conflicting evidence. For example, you might find that your dreams predict real events. However, this is only because you actually forget most of your dreams unless an event happens to remind you of them. Therefore the fact that you think dreams are evidence of precognition is only because you forget all those instances when it was not true.

Blackmore (1992) has explained psi-phenomena as a form of cognitive illusion – we are used to the idea that things have explanations and therefore seek to provide one. At least 'sheep' do; 'goats' accept that some things are simply random coincidences and are not caused by anything. In an experiment where people were asked to generate random numbers it was shown that 'goats' are better at this than 'sheep', in other words 'goats' cope better with the concept of randomness.

Finally, I should mention the problem of publication bias. There is a tendency for psychological journals to publish only positive results and the studies which report no significance are rejected. This misrepresents the actual research which has taken place and produces a bias in favour of the existence of psi-phenomena.

I hope you find all this of interest and that it leads you to question the evidence more closely.

Yours, in no doubt.

Examiner's tip The reply includes a wealth of arguments against the existence of paranormal phenomena. The evidence is coherently presented and well detailed. A good answer should contain at least three points and include at least two empirical studies. An answer which includes only one study or one point would receive a maximum of 3 marks.

Question 2

Examiner's tip You should tailor your answer to the available marks for each section. Part (a) should be brief and part (b)(i) requires less than part (b)(ii). In part (b) make sure that the theories/empirical evidence are firmly set in the context of motivation and job satisfaction. There is considerable overlap between these so take care not to use the same evidence twice.

(a) Absenteeism is absence from work or a planned activity for any length of time, and this includes lateness. Two explanations are illness and unhappiness at work.

Examiner's tip The definition contains some detail and therefore is worth 2 marks; a definition which lacks detail would only receive 1 mark. The further 2 marks are awarded for two explanations which are relevant. You should avoid tautologies such as 'Absenteeism is when you are absent'. Other explanations which could have been used include: domestic problems, boredom, stress, and lack of job satisfaction.

(b) (i)   Two factors which may encourage people to work are the need for achievement or self-actualization, and the pleasantness of their job.

McClelland has proposed a theory that people vary in their needs for different things, notably achievement. If someone has a high need for achievement (nAch) this will lead to a desire to work. There are six components of nAch: work ethic, pursuit of excellence, status aspiration, competitiveness, acquisitiveness and mastery. There is some evidence that this approach has a male bias and does not predict achievement in women very well.

Examiner's tip   Where possible include this kind of evaluation because it is evidence of critical understanding.

Maslow wrote about a hierarchy of needs where self-actualization is the highest need. It is only motivating if a person has satisfied their lower needs, such as food and security. There are middle range needs, such as for belongingness and esteem, both of which may be motivating factors for work. Maslow predicted that the needs at a particular level stop being motivating when they are filled and then the needs at the next level up become motivating. If lower needs become unfilled then the person will concentrate on them. Money is important in securing basic needs so that if a worker has little money they will not be concerned with the need for achievement. This theory has the advantage of being a general theory of motivation.

Job design theories suggest that people may want to work more if their job is well designed. Hackman and Oldham (1976) proposed three dimensions for a good job. First, that the work should be perceived as meaningful. Second, people should be given a greater sense of responsibility. Third, they should have feedback, in the form of knowing the results of their labour. Without these a worker will feel dissatisfied and lose the desire to work.

Examiner's tip   A very thorough answer which covers three rather than the required two factors because McClelland's and Maslow's accounts are substantially different. Only two factors would count towards the final mark. Alternative theoretical accounts include Alderfer's ERG theory and Schein's social approach.

Answers which do not explicitly use theoretical accounts would be limited to a maximum of 3 marks. If only one theory is cited then the maximum mark would be 4.

(ii)   Certain strategies will increase an individual's job satisfaction. These may be related to intrinsic factors of the job itself, or related to working conditions.

One way of increasing satisfaction is to improve the job itself. Job enrichment is a motivational programme which aims to give workers more involvement in their jobs so they feel less bored. This can be done by giving them a greater role in planning and evaluating their jobs. Janson (1971) found that typists improve their production rates when they are asked to correct their own mistakes.

An alternative is to provide workers with specific and achievable incentives. Goal-setting theory states that people need goals which they can achieve. Piecework is an example of this, where a worker is paid in relation to what they produce. Group piecework may be even better because it encourages co-operation and reduces conflicts. The problem with this theory is that piecework may increase satisfaction but it may not lead to high quality work.

Job satisfaction can be related to the fit between the worker and their job. Carlson (1966) found that workers who had a large mismatch between their abilities and the requirements of their job, did not get satisfaction from good

performance. This is probably because you can only feel satisfied about doing something you regard as appropriate to your self-image.

Job satisfaction can also be related to working conditions rather than the job itself. Greater satisfaction can be achieved by paying people more or changing the way that they are paid, for example, performance-related bonuses or profit-sharing schemes. Workers can be offered various benefits aside from direct pay such as good pension schemes, child care or medical insurance. If the work place is pleasant this will increase satisfaction. This can be achieved by having smaller workgroups to improve social relationships and a clean, well-decorated work environment with minimal noise.

The structure of the organization may affect the way people feel. For example, a bureaucracy where there is poor communication between the bottom and the top decreases satisfaction. Whereas the Japanese style of management which emphasizes interdependence and encourages worker participation in decision making will increase satisfaction.

Herzberg (1966) proposed a two-factor theory: job satisfaction and job dissatisfaction. He interviewed 200 professionals and found that job satisfaction came from 'motivators', things like responsibility, recognition and achievement. Dissatisfaction came from 'hygienes' which are things like working conditions, pay levels and benefits. It is not enough to pay attention to hygienes or motivators, they both need to be OK in order to motivate the work force.

Warr (1987) proposed a vitamin model – there are some attributes which produce constantly positive effects (like vitamin C), for example, money, physical security and valued social position. There are other factors which are toxic if excessive (like vitamin A): variety, control and interpersonal contact. We need minimum daily amounts of the good vitamins and limited amounts of the toxic ones.

Examiner's tip It is important that this answer is not just an essay about theories of job satisfaction, but attempts to provide reasons related to job satisfaction. It is the fullness of the answer which is important and the use of both theory and research. If there is no reference to empirical studies the maximum mark would be 5. A middle band answer (4–7 marks) will use both theory and research but will not produce a convincing argument. There may be a limited number of strategies mentioned and/or only one or two empirical studies and theories. A weak answer (1–3 marks) will make little reference to either theory or research and the discussion will be anecdotal.

Question 3

Examiner's tip You should note that this question is not related to the causes of pain but rather to ways of managing and controlling it. In part (a) you are asked to describe a number of studies or approaches. Your description should use psychological terminology in a detailed manner and communicate understanding.

In part (b) you should use the 'HINT' to guide your answer; for the studies/approaches mentioned consider their effectiveness, the methodologies, perspectives and related ethical issues. Remember that criticism can be positive as well as negative, and that your account should be as wide ranging as possible.

In part (c) you are asked to apply your knowledge to the issue of a coping strategy. Your answer should be detailed and appropriate. It should only concern one strategy and acute rather than chronic pain.

(a) Psychologists have suggested various ways that the problem of pain can be managed. Cognitive approaches generally aim to alter the way a person thinks about the pain. One example of this is thinking that the pain is doing some good; such redefinition should make it feel better. Melzack and Wall's (1982) gate control theory of pain explains how cognitive control works. This is that pain is only perceived when a metaphorical gate is open in the spinal cord so that the brain receives the sensory signals. This gate is 'closed' by messages descending from the brain, by the amount of activity in the pain fibres, or by other external messages. It explains, for example, why you may not notice that you cut yourself while you are doing some strenuous work but it hurts a lot afterwards. It also explains how emotional state, expectations and/or experience can alter the perception of pain.

Physical approaches treat pain through the use of drugs (e.g. morphine or an anaesthetic) or other physical methods (such as surgery or TENS). There are numerous physical therapies, for instance relaxation which decreases tension and thus reduces pain which is aggravated by tension. Acupuncture is another physical technique which may cause the release of endorphins. These are naturally occurring opiates which are the body's own form of pain killer. TENS (trans electrical nerve stimulation) is used by women in childbirth to reduce pain. This also causes the production of endorphins.

A third approach is behaviour therapy. In this case operant conditioning techniques are used to alter existing learned associations between pain and an aversive stimulus, such as helping a child to overcome a fear of injections. This is related to the cognitive approach of changing beliefs but works on behaviour rather than the way the person thinks about the event. Biofeedback techniques use this approach, which involves learning voluntary control of involuntary muscles or voluntary muscles which are not normally controlled. This is done through feedback from physiological monitoring devices.

Finally, insight therapies aim to change how the whole person feels as well as thinks. A chronic pain sufferer often becomes depressed or takes on the sick role and this makes everything worse. Counselling or group therapy may enable the person to manage the pain and their lives more effectively.

> **Examiner's tip** A number of concepts/theories have been described, each with some elaboration, detail and good use of psychological terminology. The answer demonstrates understanding and an appreciation of some wider issues. A weak answer would lack detail and understanding.
> The question could have been answered by considering different means of pain relief (depleting synaptic transmitters, stimulating the neural system which inhibits it, cognitive control) rather than via therapeutic approaches.

(b) We can evaluate the approaches listed above through a consideration of their effectiveness. There is empirical support for the effectiveness of the cognitive approach. For example, Wernick (1983) showed that patients with severe burns reduced their medication if they were given a greater sense of self-control. Expectations and beliefs about pain have been shown to affect the perception of pain. For example, Kent (1985) found that anxious dental patients estimated pain as more severe three months after treatment than they had before the treatment. This supports the idea that expectations are more important than the actual experience. Therefore if you change the person's expectations they should experience less pain.

The use of drugs has been criticized in terms of their side effects and risk to life. They are not very good for chronic pain because of addiction problems. It is possible that drugs work because people expect them to, a placebo effect. Levine *et al.* (1978) showed how the fact that people think they are taking a painkiller produces endorphins. They gave patients a placebo injection before dental treatment and then an injection of naloxone after (naloxone blocks endorphins). When the patients were given naloxone their pain increased showing that the placebo had led to the production of endorphins.

Behaviour therapies have been shown to be very effective in the treatment of pain. One example is some research by Cogan *et al.* (197) who found that subjects were able to tolerate 50% more pain when they listened to a recording of Lily Tomlin than in a relaxation group or when listening to an educational lecture.

Biofeedback has some empirical support. For example, Miller (1969) taught rats to alter their heart rates by rewarding the animals whenever their heart rates changed in the desired direction (operant conditioning). To stop the rats using their voluntary chest muscles they were paralysed with curare. There has not been much success replicating this, though some experiments with humans have shown how they can be trained to control unused voluntary muscles.

The evidence cited here concentrates on one kind of pain problem, treatment in clinics or hospital. It is difficult to know how this might be generalized to the management of pain in more ordinary situations such as having a headache or banging your elbow. The research also could be explained in terms of the Hawthorne effect: some of the patients may have been responding to the additional attention they were receiving from researchers and therefore felt more positive about their pain.

An important consideration in relation to all these approaches is whether they are ethical. The use of drugs or surgery without a patient's consent is unethical. They should be able to give their informed consent but in some cases doctors themselves do not know all the side effects. If a drug is experimental it should not be tested on humans, though some patients might prefer to have some treatment rather than suffer chronic pain especially if they have a terminal illness.

Examiner's tip   A number of criteria have been used to evaluate the approaches described in part (a). The discussion is clearly related to pain management. There is some attempt to consider the quality of the evidence and ethical issues. The answer shows an awareness of the strengths and weaknesses rather than just focusing on negative criticism.
A weaker answer would mention only one or two criteria and lack scope and detail.

(c) One example of acute rather than chronic pain would be the pain you have when a dentist drills your tooth. An appropriate cognitive coping strategy would be to imagine the pain as something constructive and associate it with nice things. This is why dentists put nice pictures on their walls. It is a form of cognitive redefinition and is similar to relaxation as a coping strategy because it leads to relaxation, but it seeks to alter the sensation of pain not just by relaxing you but also by making the person have different expectations.

A number of empirical studies have supported the effectiveness of cognitive redefinition. Basler and Rehfisch (1990) trained patients with pain to reinterpret their pain experience, avoid negative thinking and use distraction at key times. These patients reported less pain and visited the doctor less than a control group. The study was actually related to chronic pain but the findings are relevant to acute pain as well.

The importance of expectations is shown in Seligman's work on learned helplessness because this shows how previous bad experiences lead to the presumption that the same will occur next time. When someone finds they have no control over pain they learn to accept it and have a continued expectation of having no control. This means that they give in to future pain experiences, in this case a trip to the dentist, and assume that it will hurt.

Examiner's tip The answer given is detailed and accurate. It is difficult to provide a great deal of material since you are limited to applying one coping strategy. A weaker answer would tend towards the anecdotal and lack detail.

Question 4

Examiner's tip In part (a) you should ensure that the two styles you select are different otherwise you will not receive full marks and you will have difficulty with part (b). For this second part you must avoid an anecdotal answer, tempting in an area where students feel competent to offer unsubstantiated opinions – you are warned to 'refer to theory and empirical evidence in your answer'. The key issues will be reward, discipline and

Outline answer for part (a)

There are two dimensions along which styles vary, you should select one from each:

- Name one of: teacher-centred, formal, didactic, authoritarian, direct, traditional approaches. Description: emphasis on the group, on assessment, on staying in your seat, on a body of facts conveyed by an expert.
- Name one of: pupil-centred, discovery, indirect, democratic, informal, progressive methods. Description: the approach is centred on the pupil's needs and readiness, on group work, on student freedom, on self-directed activity, not on assessment.

Examiner's tip You would receive 2 marks for two named approaches which are *different* and 2 marks for each good description.

Outline answer for part (b)

1 How teacher-centred approaches affect students' motivation:

- They use extrinsic rewards, e.g. praise, gold stars, good grades. Brophy (1981): praise should be informative, creditable and not too frequent. Extrinsic rewards may be counterproductive. Lepper *et al.* (1973): intrinsic rewards more effective than extrinsic ones.
- They use punishment, which may be counterproductive in motivating students. Punishments habituate or lead to a desire to rebel. Some see it as dehumanizing and mechanistic, like training animals. The same principles of conditioning may not be appropriate for humans.
- They use assessment/feedback. This is more likely to be summative: pupils motivated by threat of terminal assessment. It is also more likely to extrinsic: supplied by others.
- They use power relationships to motivate pupils: this may alienate some pupils.

2 How pupil-centred approaches affect students' motivation:

- They use intrinsic rewards more than extrinsic ones: Piaget – students motivate themselves and this makes learning more effective. Maslow –

hierarchy of needs, self-actualization drives people forward to learn. White – competence motivation.

- They use some punishment: more likely to be authoritative rather than authoritarian, i.e. use reason rather than power.

- They use some assessment/feedback: student will be self-motivated without assessment, more likely to be formative, pupils motivated by continual feedback, more likely to be intrinsic feedback: self-assessment.

3   Other considerations:

- Individual differences: some people better motivated by teacher-centred approach because they lack self-direction.

- There are many overlaps between the two approaches, e.g. use of praise.

- Each approach is related to different aims: teacher-centred approach emphasizes curriculum content whereas pupil-centred approach is concerned with personal development and self-direction as well as knowledge.

Examiner's tip   A good answer (top band) will provide a comprehensive account of the ways that your two named teaching styles affect motivation, supported by several psychological theories and/or research. It will communicate a realistic understanding of the behaviours linked to each teaching method. A weak answer will make little reference to psychological concepts and only outline some positive and negative factors.

Question 5

Examiner's tip   In part (a) you are asked to 'review' relevant psychological studies and then evaluate them in part (b) in terms of their conclusions and methodologies, as well as in relation to ethical issues and psychological perspectives. All material related to crowd behaviour must apply to emergency situations. Part (c) gives you the opportunity to apply your knowledge.

Outline answer for part (a)

Key studies:

- Darley and Latané (1968): students listened to other group members over an intercom, one member became ill. Subjects less likely to help when there were other helpers.

- Latané and Darley (1968): subjects answered questionnaire and room filled with smoke. The more people present the longer it took someone to report the emergency.

- Clark and Word (1972): subjects filled out a questionnaire during which they heard a crash followed by silence (high ambiguity) or groans (low ambiguity). They all helped in low ambiguity no matter how many others present.

- Piliavin *et al.* (1969): passengers on N.Y. subway more likely to help victim with a cane than one who appeared drunk. Also found that men more likely to help and that people more likely to help members of the same race.

- Bickman (1974): left dime in phone box. People more likely to help someone wearing a suit than one wearing unkempt work clothes.

- Beaman *et al.* (1978): showed that people more likely to help after they had heard a lecture or film about helping behaviour.

- Bryan and Test (1967): motorists were more likely to help someone with a flat tyre if they saw someone else doing the same thing earlier on.

> **Examiner's tip** Four or five studies would be sufficient for a top band answer. Marks are awarded for the use of appropriate and accurately described evidence, as well as the use of psychological terminology.
> A weak answer would lack detail and understanding.

Outline answer for part (b)

(i) Their conclusions: all studies showed aspects of the bystander effect, that people often do not help in emergency situations.

- Darley and Latané = diffusion of responsibility.
- Latané and Darley = pluralistic ignorance.
- Clark and Word = effects of ambiguity.
- Piliavin *et al.* = diffusion of responsibility effect reversed because it was clearly an emergency and they could see that no one else was helping.
- Piliavin *et al.* and Bickman = helping behaviour influenced by characteristics of the victim.
- Beaman *et al.* and Bryan and Test = prosocial models may decrease the bystander effect.

(ii) Their methodologies:

- Laboratory experiment, e.g. Darley and Latané, Latané and Darley, Clark and Word. Negative: studies lack real life validity, open to experimenter effects. Positive: good control of variables, can be replicated.
- Field experiment, e.g. Piliavin *et al.*, Beaman *et al.* and Bryan and Test. Negative: more expensive and time-consuming, less control therefore less sure about causal factors, still subject to some experimental problems such as sample bias and experimenter effects. Positive: more like real life.

(iii) Ethical questions:

- Field experiments deny participants rights such as informed consent and debriefing.
- All experiments involve deception, therefore participants cannot give informed consent.
- All experiments may create distress in subjects.

(iv) Psychological perspectives:

- The behaviourist perspective would say that helping behaviour is due to the experience of rewards and punishment.
- Social learning theory would suggest that we learn helping behaviour through vicarious reinforcement and modelling our behaviour on others (Beaman *et al.*, Bryan and Test).
- The ethological perspective would suggest that we have innate predispositions to behave altruistically (kin selection). Reciprocal altruism is a way of ensuring that you will be helped in the future.
- The cognitive perspective would emphasize the role of expectations and beliefs, e.g. pluralistic ignorance and costs of intervening.

Examiner's tip A number of criteria should be used to evaluate the quality of the evidence, and these criteria should be wide ranging and detailed. The answer should show an awareness of the strengths and weaknesses rather than just focusing on negative criticism. A weaker answer would mention only one or two criteria and lack scope and detail.

Outline answer for part (c)

Your message should aim to:

- Avoid diffusion of responsibility. Speak to each individual. Prevent individuals feeling it is not their problem or responsibility. People often do not help because they think the problem is not theirs.

- Avoid pluralistic ignorance. Instruct certain individuals to act as a models for others to follow.

- Avoid effects of ambiguity. Be very clear about what people should do and not do. It will help to repeat the message many times.

- Avoid lack of empathy. If people sympathize with other victims they may be more prepared to help.

- Encourage co-operation and calmness and be authoritative.

Examiner's tip In this part of the question you should demonstrate how you can apply the psychological knowledge outlined in parts (a) and (b) to a real situation. Make sure that your message contains elements which are related to the previous psychological evidence. The answer should be accurate, detailed and wide ranging. A weaker answer would tend towards the anecdotal and lack detail.

Acknowledgements

The author would like to thank officers of the examination boards for their support and assistance: Margaret Heritage, Elspeth Wagstaff and their staff. Fellow examiners have been most helpful in offering advice and editing the text: especial thanks to Mike Cardwell, Roger Davies and Anthony Curtis.

The author and publishers gratefully acknowledge the following examination boards for permission to use questions in this book: Questions 1, 3, 4 (Unit 1); 2, 3, 4 (Unit 2); 1, 2, 3, 4 (Unit 3); 4 (Unit 4); 1, 2, 3, 4 (Unit 5); 1, 2, 3, 4 (Unit 6); 1, 2, 3 (Unit 7) and 2 (Unit 8): Reproduced by kind permission of the Associated Examining Board. Any answers or hints on answers are the sole responsibility of the author and have not been provided or approved by the Board. Questions 3 (Unit 4); 4 (Unit 8) and 1, 2, 4 (Unit 9): Reproduced by kind permission of the Northern Examinations and Assessment Board. The author accepts responsibility for answers provided, which may not necessarily constitute the only possible solutions. Questions 3, 5 (Unit 9): Reproduced by kind permission of the Oxford and Cambridge Schools Examination Board. The board bears no responsibility for the example answers to questions taken from its past question papers which are contained in this publication.

108